ARTIST
OF THE
REVOLUTION

To every noble cause your heart
Went forth unerring, true,
Maybe you played a greater part,
And braver than you knew.

Maeve Cavanagh

ARTIST
OF THE
REVOLUTION

THE CARTOONS OF ERNEST KAVANAGH

(1884–1916)

JAMES CURRY

MERCIER PRESS
IRISH PUBLISHER – IRISH STORY

To the memory of my father James.
Thanks Dad.

MERCIER PRESS
Cork
www.mercierpress.ie

© Text: James Curry, 2012
© Images: National Library of Ireland

ISBN: 978 1 85635 948 1

10 9 8 7 6 5 4 3 2 1

A CIP record for this title is available from the British Library

Printed and bound in the EU.

Contents

Abbreviations

BMH WS	–	Bureau of Military History Witness Statement
CSORP	–	Chief Secretary's Office Registered Papers
DMP	–	Dublin Metropolitan Police
ICA	–	Irish Citizen Army
ITGWU	–	Irish Transport and General Workers' Union
IWWU	–	Irish Women Workers' Union
MP	–	Member of Parliament
NA	–	National Archives of Ireland
NLI	–	National Library of Ireland
RIC	–	Royal Irish Constabulary

Acknowledgements

I would like to thank Charles Callan, L. Perry Curtis Jr, Vera Kreilkamp, Felix M. Larkin, Charlie Maguire, Theresa Moriarty, Emmet O'Connor and Pádraig Yeates for taking the time to read draft sections of my research at various stages of its completion and providing me with valuable feedback; Francis Devine for also providing me with helpful feedback and generously supplying me with an unpublished conference paper which he had written on Ernest Kavanagh's cartoons; Eunan O'Halpin for pointing me in the right direction with regards to important archival sources; Marnie Hay for helpful comments regarding the two cartoons featuring Bulmer Hobson which are included in this book; Stephen MacEoin for supplying me with material from the Military Archives; the staff at the Dublin City Library and Archive; Trinity College Dublin Library, especially Lorcan O'Meara, Brendan Byrne and Anthony O'Rourke; and the National Library of Ireland, in particular Bernie Metcalfe for allowing me access to the library's hardcopy edition of *The Irish Worker*; and Gerry Kavanagh for assisting me above and beyond the call of duty and enthusiastically spreading the word about his cartoonist namesake. My thanks also to Sandra Hartwieg for allowing me to avail of her photographic expertise and offering me continual encouragement; to Kevin Fetherston for helping me with genealogical research; and to Philip Curry, Jack McGinley and Tanya Whittaker for their helpful advice. Finally, I would like to thank my mother, Ann Curry, for putting up with me during the writing of this book; and Mary Feehan and the rest of the staff at Mercier Press for placing their faith in me.

I would also like to thank the National Library of Ireland for permission to reproduce all of the images in this book, including images from *Cartoons. Ernest Kavanagh ('E.K.') of 'The Worker'*

(Dublin 1918) which is contained in the William O'Brien Papers (Ms 33, 718/c(107)), as well as the following:

- 'Time to do this' by Gordon Brewster, published on page 1 of the *Evening Herald* on 6 September 1913.
- 'Strike at the Haul' by W. J. Miller, published on page 5 of *The Liberator and Irish Trade Unionist* on 6 September 1913.
- 'The Call to Arms' by Maeve Cavanagh, published on page 8 of *The Workers' Republic* on 8 April 1916.
- 'Ernest Cavanagh. Easter Tuesday 1916' by Maeve Cavanagh, published on page 1 of *Irish Opinion: Voice of Labour* on 19 April 1919.
- 'James Connolly, IRA' by Maeve Cavanagh, *A Voice of Insurgency* (Dublin 1916), p. 13.
- 'To 'E.K.' by Maeve Cavanagh, *A Voice of Insurgency* (Dublin 1916), pp. 22–3.
- 'Ireland to Germany' by Maeve Cavanagh, *A Voice of Insurgency* (Dublin 1916), p. 43.
- 'Ireland's overture to Germany' by Maeve Cavanagh, *A Voice of Insurgency* (Dublin 1916), p. 48.
- 'In Brave '16' by Maeve Cavanagh, *Passion Flowers* (Dublin 1918), p. 24.
- 'The Menace' by Maeve Cavanagh, published on page 2 of *The Irish Worker* on 26 April 1913.
- 'Leaderless' by Maeve Cavanagh, published on page 2 of *The Irish Worker* on 10 August 1912.

INTRODUCTION

On the morning of 25 April 1916, Ernest Kavanagh was shot dead on the front steps of Liberty Hall, the headquarters of the Irish Transport and General Workers' Union (ITGWU) where he was employed as a clerk. One of several hundred civilians to be killed during the Easter Rising, Kavanagh was thirty-two years old at the time of his death.[1]

Attempts by Kavanagh's family to secure the opening of an inquiry into his killing predictably ended in failure. The British government, when questioned on the matter at Westminster in the months afterwards, repeatedly refused to launch an investigation into his death. On 3 July Irish MP Laurence Ginnell pressed Prime Minister Herbert Asquith on the need for a 'public inquiry into the shooting of non-combatant civilians by the military in Dublin' during the Easter Rising, listing Kavanagh's name among the Eden Quay victims who had been killed while going about 'their peaceful pursuits at the time'. Asquith replied that there was no plan to launch any inquiry since his government had not received any information about 'the casualties in Eden Quay', whom, he assumed, had perished during 'the bombardment of Liberty Hall, a rebel stronghold'.[2] When the House of Commons resumed the following week Ginnell continued his efforts to secure justice for the Eden

---

1   Ernest Kavanagh was born in Dublin on 16 January 1884 at his Wentworth Place home. At the time of his death he was still living with his family in the city, at an address on Ranelagh's Oxford Road, having earlier lived at Desmond Street in Dublin's Wood Quay district.
2   *Hansard Parliamentary Debates. Fifth Series – Vol. LXXXIII* (London 1916), 3 July 1916.

Quay victims, asking Asquith if 'the fact that the area comprises Liberty Hall' was enough to deprive their relatives of 'the right of inquiry which they would otherwise have?' The prime minister responded with a declaration that 'such information as I have received does not lead me to think any inquiry is called for in this matter'. When challenged by Ginnell on these words, Asquith added that 'certainly one, if not two' of the Eden Quay casualties had been 'shot by the rebels'.[3]

Arthur Lynch was another Irish MP who campaigned for justice on Ernest Kavanagh's behalf. On 3 July Lynch specifically highlighted Kavanagh's death as worthy of a government inquiry:

> This young man, though he had taken no part whatever in the Rising, was shot while alone, unarmed, and defenceless on the steps of Liberty Hall, under conditions which gave no ground for supposing that he was a combatant.[4]

Having received the reply from Herbert Samuel, a leading member of the British cabinet, that no information was known about Kavanagh's death, Lynch agreed to forward the evidence he possessed about the shooting. He then returned to Westminster ten days later, asking:

> whether an inquiry will be set on foot to ascertain the circumstances in which Ernest Kavanagh met his death on 25th April on the steps of Liberty Hall, Dublin; and, if so, whether the statements of his relatives will be tested, to the effect that Ernest Kavanagh was never a member of any organisation which advocated physical force, that he was absent on a holiday during four days preceding the Rising, that having been employed as a clerk in the State

---

3   *Ibid., Vol. LXXXIV*, 11 July 1916.
4   *Ibid., Vol. LXXXIII*, 3 July 1916.

insurance section of the Irish Transport Workers' Union he had gone, on Tuesday, 25th April, to Liberty Hall to ascertain whether the staff was still there, that he was shot and killed while alone and unarmed, that the shots came from the Customs House nearby, and that no warning was given?[5]

Relying on information he had received from the Dublin Metropolitan Police (DMP), that Kavanagh had been 'accidently shot outside Liberty Hall by a member of the [Irish] Citizen Army' on Easter Monday, Samuel refused to open an inquiry.[6] He remained firm even after receiving the following amended police report about Kavanagh from Dublin a few days later:

> So far as can be ascertained from inquiry … appears to have been shot when attempting to enter Liberty Hall about 10 a.m. on Tuesday, 25th April, 1916, and not on Monday 24th, as previously stated. It is not known by whom he was shot, although at the time of the occurrence it was rumoured that he was accidentally shot outside Liberty Hall, and at the time there were a number of Sinn Féiners in the latter place from which they were firing on the military.[7]

When parliament resumed that same day and Lynch called for the British government to make public the evidence that Kavanagh 'was shot by a member of the Irish Citizen Army', Samuel, although still maintaining that there was no need for an inquiry to be launched, now had a different story to report:

> The answer which I gave to the Hon. Member on the 13th July was based on information obtained by the police. They were not present when Kavanagh was killed, as no police were on duty on the streets at the time, but the information was believed to be accurate.

---

5   *Ibid.*, 13 July 1916.
6   National Archives of Ireland, CSORP, 25329/1916.
7   *Ibid.*

After further investigation the police report that, so far as can be ascertained, Kavanagh was shot when attempting to enter Liberty Hall on the morning of the 25th April, and not on the 24th, as previously stated. No troops were operating in this area on the 24th, but by the time at which it now appears Kavanagh was killed, the rebels in Liberty Hall and the military in the Custom House were firing at one another, so it is not possible to say definitely by whom he was shot.[8]

On 27 July Lynch made one last effort on Kavanagh's behalf, when he urged the British government to request that the DMP consult with the military stationed in Dublin 'so that, as the police were not themselves present, every means of ascertaining the truth may be made'.[9] Although Samuel agreed to this request, it was to prove in vain. Shortly afterwards a report from Dublin Castle effectively shut the case on Kavanagh's shooting by revealing:

Firing was going on in the locality on the 25th April ... If this man was standing at or passing Liberty Hall he would probably have been fired at, by the Citizen Army if he did not belong to them, or by the Military if he was not on Military duty.[10]

It was never mentioned in any of these debates that Ernest Kavanagh was actually an established political cartoonist at the time of his death, having contributed dozens of hard-hitting illustrations to Irish labour, nationalist and suffrage newspapers under the monogram 'E.K.' during the previous four years, several of which were reprinted in English and American publications. Although his work would occasionally appear in newspapers

---

8   *Hansard, Vol. LXXXIV*, 19 July 1916.
9   *Ibid.*, 27 July 1916.
10 National Archives of Ireland, CSORP, 25329/1916.

such as *Fianna*, *Irish Freedom* and the *Irish Citizen*, it was his prolific series of cartoons for the ITGWU's official weekly paper that saw Kavanagh gain the most notoriety.

The Irish Worker newspaper

The launch of *The Irish Worker and People's Advocate* on 27 May 1911 saw James Larkin, the newspaper's editor, fulfil a long-held ambition. In the first issue of the weekly publication, which appeared every Saturday and later had its title shortened to simply *The Irish Worker*, Larkin explained the reason for its existence: 'Too long, aye! far too long, have we, the Irish working people been humble and inarticulate,' he declared, before expressing his belief that the written word was 'the most potent force in our modern world'.[11] The implication was clear: the playing field for the propaganda war regarding the ever-increasing industrial unrest in Ireland had finally been levelled.[12] The ITGWU saw the founding of *The Irish Worker* as 'epoch-making' and championed its existence as the only paper in Ireland 'advocating the principles of the common people, articulating their grievances, and voicing their demands'.[13] Historians have likewise largely proved willing to shower the paper with praise, describing it as 'an amazing success',[14] 'less a newspaper than the spirit of four glorious

---

11 *The Irish Worker*, 27 May 1911.

12 Previous short-lived attempts to establish a labour paper in Ireland included the *Cork Trades and Labour Journal* (1908), *Dublin Trades and Labour Journal* (1909) and, more successfully, the *Belfast Labour Chronicle* (1904–6).

13 See Francis Devine, *Organising History: A Centenary of SIPTU* (Dublin 2009), p. 48.

14 R. M. Fox, *Jim Larkin: The Rise of the Underman* (New York 1957), p. 73.

years',[15] 'something unprecedented in any city in the world',[16] 'extraordinary ... a milestone in the history of working-class journalism'[17] and 'in every way ... Larkin's triumph'.[18] Even one early critic, specifically commissioned to present the employers' side of the story regarding the Dublin Lockout, was under no illusions about its contemporary and historical importance. Arnold Wright noted that the paper, which he routinely condemned, could not be 'too carefully studied by anyone who would obtain a true perception of what the Larkinite labour movement is, and by what means it is kept alive'.[19]

The working class of Ireland responded to the paper with enthusiasm. When addressing the paper's circulation figures for its first year of publication, labour historian William P. Ryan, writing in 1919, claimed that it had sold 26,000 copies in June, 66,500 copies in July, 74,750 copies in August, and 94,994 copies in September.[20] These were extraordinarily high numbers for the time, which Ryan claimed might have been even greater had the paper's printing machinery been more advanced. The fact that he failed to cite his source when providing these figures has not prevented many historians from accepting the validity of Ryan's

---

15 Emmet Larkin, *James Larkin, Irish labour leader, 1876–1947* (London 1965), p. 76.

16 C. D. Greaves, *The Irish Transport and General Workers' Union: the formative years 1909–1923* (Dublin 1982), p. 57.

17 Robert Lowery, 'Sean O'Casey and *The Irish Worker* (with an index, 1911–14)' in Robert Lowery (ed.), *O'Casey Annual 3* (London 1984), p. 34.

18 Emmet O'Connor, *James Larkin* (Cork 2002), p. 32.

19 Arnold Wright, *Disturbed Dublin: the story of the great strike of 1913–14: with a description of the industries of the Irish capital* (London 1914), p. 52.

20 W. P. Ryan, *The Irish labour movement from the 'twenties to our own day* (Dublin 1919), p. 197.

numbers or, for that matter, misinterpreting them as weekly rather than monthly sales. In actual fact, they were taken from a flysheet soliciting support for the proposed Irish Co-operative Labour Press that the paper had circulated in late 1911 and which was subsequently shown to Ryan by union leader William O'Brien.[21] This flyer was signed by Larkin, who had said something similar in *The Irish Worker* at around the same time in question, claiming that the paper sold in the 'first week 5,000 copies; second week, 8,000; third week, 15,000; now upwards of 20,000 copies, and we could sell double the quantity if we could print them'.[22] *The Irish Worker* reiterated this point a few months later when it talked of weekly sales of 'approximately 20,000', although now it was reported that the circulation might conceivably be 'trebled' if the workers only helped to enable its expansion.[23] Although this may well have been true, a comparison of the existing figures suggests that 20,000 copies was more likely a reflection of the paper's best-selling issues rather than an indication of its normal circulation, which probably averaged around 14–15,000 copies.[24]

It should be made clear that such a figure would still have been hugely impressive for a publication such as *The Irish Worker*, especially since many Irish wholesalers refused to stock the paper.

21 National Library of Ireland, William O'Brien Papers, LO P 120 (2).
22 *The Irish Worker*, 21 October 1911.
23 *Ibid.*, 9 March 1912.
24 For example, in June 1911 *The Irish Worker* produced four issues which apparently sold, according to Ryan's figures, some 26,000 copies. Such a number would seem far below an educated estimate should one believe Larkin's contemporaneous claim that the first two issues of the month had sold 23,000 copies (i.e. 'second week, 8000; third week, 15,000') between them. Furthermore, *The Irish Times* revealed on 27 August 1913 that the paper had sold approximately 14,000 copies the previous week and had a circulation which varied between 8,000 to 22,000.

To put the achievement into context, Sinn Féin's weekly paper was selling less than 5,000 copies at the time,[25] a figure that itself far exceeded the circulation of most 'seditious and disloyal' Irish newspapers in the months leading up to the Easter Rising.[26] In light of the overcrowding amongst Dublin's working-class population at the time, it needs also to be remembered that the overall readership of *The Irish Worker* would undoubtedly have been significantly higher, with families and work colleagues invariably sharing the paper around.[27]

Larkin relied on a network of writers to negate, as Robert Lowery expressed it, 'the instability which is found in any radical paper which challenges the status quo or relies on the dependency of one person'.[28] Among the most prolific contributors to the paper were James Connolly, Sean O'Casey, William P. Partridge, Delia Larkin (younger sister of James) and Standish O'Grady. The paper followed a basic four broadsheet page style that remained in place throughout the course of its existence, with the exception of a couple of issues. Such a format meant that the problem of space restrictions regularly cropped up with articles continually 'held over until our next issue' or spread out over several weeks. Nonetheless, in spite of this logistical drawback *The Irish Worker*

---

25 See Virginia E. Glandon, *Arthur Griffith and the Advanced-Nationalist Press in Ireland, 1900–1922* (New York 1985), p. 45.

26 Breandán Mac Giolla Choille (ed.), *Intelligence Notes 1913–16* (Dublin 1966), pp. 162–3.

27 The *Report of the Department Committee appointed by the Local Government Board for Ireland to Inquire into the Housing Condition of the Working Classes in the City of Dublin* (Dublin 1914) revealed that 87,305 people making up some 25,822 families lived in the city's 5,322 tenement buildings, many of which were deemed to be 'unfit for habitation'.

28 Lowery, 'Sean O'Casey and *The Irish Worker*', p. 41.

managed to cram a wealth of content into its quartet of pages each week, nearly always including at least one item sure to spark controversy and set tongues wagging across Dublin. Speaking during his American trial for 'criminal anarchy' in April 1920, Larkin declared that his life's work had been to 'get the truth and put it in language so that all men can understand it' rather than assuming literary airs and appearing as a great theoretician.[29] This transparency of expression was a defining characteristic of *The Irish Worker* and undoubtedly contributed greatly to its success. As R. M. Fox observed, Larkin did not have 'the slightest interest in theory' regarding his editorship of the paper, instead adapting a 'smashing technique' to ensure readers understood his message at all times.[30]

Although a host of targets came under fire in its pages, the most striking recipient of abuse was William Martin Murphy, Ireland's leading businessman of the era and the man who became Larkin's ultimate nemesis. In addition to controlling the *Irish Independent*, *Evening Herald* and *Irish Catholic* newspapers, Murphy owned the Dublin United Tramway Company, a selection of large hotels and drapery businesses across the city, 'and God knows what else besides' to quote playwright Sean O'Casey.[31] He also had international foreign investments that stretched as far afield as Africa and South America.[32] And if Larkin was viciously attacked in Murphy's pages – 'mean thief',

---

29 See Dublin Labour History Workshop, *Larkin in Perspective: from communism to evolutionary socialism* (Dublin 1983), p. 5.

30 Fox, *Jim Larkin*, p. 74.

31 Sean O'Casey, *Autobiographies I* (London 1963), p. 576.

32 For more on Murphy see Thomas Morrissey, *William Martin Murphy* (Dundalk 1997); Dermot Keogh, 'William Martin Murphy and the origins of the 1913 Lockout' in *Saothar* 4 (1978), pp. 15–34.

'impudent, swaggering bully', 'man of ill-disciplined mind and inveterate malice' are just some examples – it was nothing in comparison to the insults hurled at Murphy by *The Irish Worker* in return. At various times Murphy was described as an 'industrial octopus', 'Tramway Tyrant', 'blood-sucking vampire', 'Whited Sepulchre', 'soulless, money-grabbing tyrant' and 'the most foul and vicious blackguard that ever polluted any country'.

Murphy was far from the only prominent businessman or public figure to receive this type of treatment. Yet whereas it was these vicious personal attacks that saw *The Irish Worker* gain notoriety and resulted in Larkin having to appear in court seven times during the paper's first year of publication alone, it was the paper's potential for inciting violence that actually posed more of a threat to its existence. On 19 August 1911 a front-page article on 'Capital and Labour' declared:

> A scab is a traitor to his class, a deserter who goes over to the enemy in time of war to fight against his own people … When a man deserts from our ranks in time of war (for a strike is war between capital and labour) he on the same principle forfeits his life to us. If England is justified in shooting those who desert to the enemy, we also are justified in killing a scab.[33]

It was these words that first brought *The Irish Worker* to the serious attention of Dublin Castle and the DMP, who inevitably monitored the paper closely over the next few years. Time and time again, however, a cautious approach was adopted by the authorities due to a fear of boosting the paper's popularity even further should unsuccessful efforts to suppress it be made. This tolerant approach allowed Larkin to make *The Irish Worker* a

---

33 *The Irish Worker*, 19 August 1911.

wonderfully scathing, defiant and controversial publication, a weapon that almost certainly helped boost membership of the ranks of the ITGWU and consolidated his popularity.

It was the crude defiance, so characteristic of *The Irish Worker*, which appealed to Belton Yearling, a fictional Protestant company director whose sympathies lay with the workers in James Plunkett's celebrated historical novel *Strumpet City*:

> One day when a copy of the Larkinite paper *The Irish Worker* was offered to him in the street, he bought it and found the style fascinating … He made a point of calling on his newsagent. There was a picket outside.
>
> 'I wish to add an extra paper to my weekly list,' he said.
>
> 'Certainly sir – which one?'
>
> '*The Irish Worker*.'
>
> 'I beg your pardon?'
>
> 'I said – *The Irish Worker*.'
>
> 'I'm afraid it is not a publication we can obtain through any of the usual distributors.'
>
> 'In that case you'll have to get it through the unusual ones, I suppose.'
>
> 'It may be difficult.'
>
> 'Not a bit,' Yearling said. 'At least twenty of them were stuck under my nose in the course of half an hour's walk through the city. There are some men prancing up and down outside your shop at this minute who, I am sure, can put you in touch with the most reliable of sources. Anyway, I am assuming you will see to it.'
>
> 'We'll do our very best, sir.'
>
> 'Thank you. In that case I know I may expect it regularly.'
>
> 'Of course, sir. Regularly. You may rely on it.'
>
> As he passed through the picket on his way out he paused to speak to the leader. 'Interesting paper you get out,' he said conversationally. 'I like the style.' They stared in unison after him.[34]

---

34 James Plunkett, *Strumpet City* (London 1969), pp. 379–80.

As Plunkett, a former branch secretary of the Workers' Union of Ireland, made clear in this scene, *The Irish Worker* was not as readily available in shops as other weekly newspapers, something which made the high sales it enjoyed all the more impressive. Larkin relied on subscription sales, word of mouth, the Dublin newsboys whom he proudly claimed received seventy-five per cent more commission than any other paper would pay, and a select group of supportive newsagents, to make *The Irish Worker* profitable. And profitable it was. On 26 August 1913 Larkin announced in court that the paper provided the ITGWU with a weekly net profit of over £8, a figure seized upon by his enemies as proof that he was exploiting the workers and growing rich at their expense, all the while forcing them to endlessly go on strike and receive a pittance in compensation from Liberty Hall.

While these attacks may have infuriated Larkin, they had little or no impact on *The Irish Worker*'s sales, with the paper continuing to thrive. Indeed, *The Irish Worker* only ceased publication following the emergence of tighter censorship regulations due to the outbreak of the First World War rather than suffering a natural demise like earlier Irish labour papers. This situation was compounded by the fact that when Larkin left Ireland for America in October 1914 he made James Connolly acting editor of *The Irish Worker* in his absence. The passing of the Defence of the Realm Act in August 1914 meant that all papers of 'doubtful loyalty' were monitored more closely than ever by Dublin Castle. When Connolly made anti-British and anti-recruitment propaganda an even more defining characteristic of *The Irish Worker* in the weeks following Larkin's departure, it was only a matter of time before the paper's days were numbered. Although *The Irish Worker*'s printer made 'certain expurgations' to its 5 December 1914 issue, these were not enough to prevent the paper contravening the new regulations and it was suppressed.[35]

Connolly tried in vain to keep the paper circulating under a different title but both *Irish Work* and *The Worker* (the name by which most people had called *The Irish Worker*) were seized upon the appearance of their first issue and immediately suppressed. The fact that *The Worker* was suppressed despite authorities recognising that it was 'socialistic and anti-capitalist', rather than 'anti-English and anti-recruiting', demonstrates how stringent wartime censorship laws in Ireland and Britain had become.[36] Faced with such a crackdown on all controversial newspapers it is difficult to see how Larkin could have succeeded in keeping *The Irish Worker* in existence even had he been in Ireland. The era of tolerance towards the ITGWU's weekly paper was over.

Looking back on its three-and-a-half year run *The Irish Worker* should be remembered as one of Larkin's greatest achievements rather than a mere libellous scandal sheet that simply got up to some mischief. Certainly, the importance of the paper was abundantly clear to the leaders of the Dublin Employers' Federation. When meeting to discuss ways in which to destroy the ITGWU before the Lockout, they laid particular stress 'upon the malign influence' exercised by *The Irish Worker* which, they argued, 'spared neither man, woman or child in pursuance of the official policy which aimed to making Mr James Larkin Dictator of the City of Dublin'.[37] One of the features of the paper most likely to infuriate the employers over the following months would undoubtedly have been the cartoons of 'E.K.'

---

35   Mac Giolla Choille, *Intelligence Notes,* p. 116.

36   *Ibid.*, p. 117.

37   Wright, *Disturbed Dublin*, p. 241.

Ernest Kavanagh's labour cartoons

The earliest that Ernest Kavanagh could have been employed as an insurance clerk at Liberty Hall is 1912, the year the National Insurance Act came into force in Ireland and an Approved Society was set up by the ITGWU at their headquarters.[38] The previous year he had been occupationally listed as a commercial clerk in the national census. A decade earlier, having completed his education at Synge Street's Christian Brothers' School, he was described in the 1901 census as an unemployed artist. The fact that he worked in Liberty Hall's insurance section may be significant in helping us to understand how he became *The Irish Worker*'s cartoonist. This was the department where Delia Larkin, general secretary of the Irish Women Workers' Union (IWWU), was also employed in a nominal capacity. Delia was *The Irish Worker*'s accountant and one of its most prolific contributors. In one of her first articles for the paper, written within weeks of its founding, she stressed *The Irish Worker*'s urgent need for 'a good cartoonist'.[39] Therefore, it is possible that it was Larkin's sister who discovered Kavanagh's artistic talents and encouraged him to contribute to the paper.[40]

In his first few months contributing to the paper Kavanagh tended to merely offer visual representations of poems. His most frequent collaborator at this time was 'Mac', the pseudonym adopted by Andrew P. Wilson, *The Irish Worker*'s sub-editor

---

38 Greaves, *Irish Transport and General Workers' Union*, p. 72.
39 *The Irish Worker*, 8 July 1911.
40 For more on Delia Larkin see Theresa Moriarty, 'Delia Larkin: Relative Obscurity' in Donal Nevin (ed.), *James Larkin: lion of the fold*, pp. 428–38; James Curry, 'Delia Larkin: More harm to the Big Fellow than any of the employers?' in *Saothar* 36 (2011), pp. 19–25.

during the paper's first two years of circulation.[41] Yet upon the outbreak of the Dublin Lockout Kavanagh's role immediately increased, and he emerged as a more independent voice whose cartoons were valued on their own merits. During this period he viciously attacked William Martin Murphy and the Dublin police on a regular basis. The DMP were frequently portrayed as brutish, bloodthirsty, drunken tyrants who were controlled by politicians and employers, and who were all too ready to administer a beating to the city's working-class population with their dreaded batons, especially if the unfortunate recipient happened to be a woman or child. Kavanagh's loathing of the Dublin police was reflected in a letter he wrote to *The Irish Worker* in May 1914 regarding a public appeal by a leader of the Irish Volunteers that all members 'assist the police in maintaining peace' during any future local disturbances that might occur. Referring to the DMP as 'murderous ruffians' and 'bloated bullies', Kavanagh declared that any man who willingly offered assistance to such people was one 'capable of any crime in the calendar'.[42]

The most obvious answer to the question of why Kavanagh used such provocative, hate-filled language and imagery with regards to the Dublin police, is that he was responding to their

---

41 The Scottish-born Andrew P. Wilson (1886–1950) contributed to *The Irish Worker* under two pseudonyms – 'Euchan' when writing prose, 'Mac' when writing poetry. Following his time at Liberty Hall, where he was a key figure in the production of *The Irish Worker* and the training of the union's drama group, he went on to become manager of the Abbey Theatre before returning to Britain and enjoying a successful television and stage career. See Steven Dedalus Burch, *Andrew P. Wilson and the Early Irish and Scottish National Theatres 1911–1950* (New York 2009).

42 *The Irish Worker*, 9 May 1914.

brutality during the opening days of the Lockout when, to use his own words, they 'butchered two of our fellow citizens and maimed hundreds of others, and spared neither woman [*sic*] or children'.[43] The key event referred to by Kavanagh was Ireland's first 'Bloody Sunday' – recently described by trade union historian Francis Devine as 'Labour's most enduring image'.[44] It was on this day that a huge gathering of police officers indiscriminately batoned hundreds of trade unionists and civilians on Sackville Street (modern-day O'Connell Street) in an orgy of violence that sent shockwaves across Ireland. Handel Booth, an MP who witnessed the carnage, later recalled the scene:

> The police had drawn their batons … It was an ordinary Sunday crowd. They were certainly bewildered, and did not know which way to turn … silence ensued save for pattering feet and sickening thuds. The noble street was in the hands of the most brutal constabulary ever let loose on a peaceful assembly … batches of the government's minions wildly striking with truncheons at every one within reach.[45]

The riot led to Dublin's main thoroughfare resembling a battle-field in a matter of minutes. The fact that the Dublin police also carried out a series of seemingly indiscriminate raids on nearby working-class homes compounded the damage to their reputation.

Thomas J. Clarke, the first signatory of the 1916 Proclamation a few short years later, expressed the indignation of many over the 'hooliganism' that occurred, writing in a letter to *The Irish Worker*:

---

43 *Ibid.*
44 Devine, *Organising History*, p. 55.
45 See Nevin, *James Larkin*, pp. 185–6.

Nothing I know of during my whole career can match the downright inhuman savagery that was witnessed recently in the streets and some of the homes of our city, when the police were let loose to run amok and indiscriminately bludgeon every man, woman and child they came across … Totting up the 'casualties' we find two dead and about a thousand maimed and battered citizens … A bloody holocaust surely! but a fitting one to be dedicated to Dublin Castle and its idea of 'Law and Order'.[46]

The Irish Worker consistently maintained that the 'hired ruffians in uniform with a lust for blood' were instruments of Dublin Castle and rich capitalists like William Martin Murphy.[47] Yet a study of Kavanagh's cartoons for the paper makes it obvious that resentment towards the Dublin police was more deep-rooted than a simple reaction to 'Bloody Sunday'. As far back as the summer of 1912, in one of his first illustrations for the paper, 'E.K.' had depicted the police as bullies who were determined to keep the working class socially suppressed by acting in cahoots with tyrannical Irish employers.[48] Such a viewpoint echoed the anti-police propaganda that regularly appeared within the print columns of *The Irish Worker*. However, what stands out is not simply Kavanagh's hatred of the police but also the manner in which he chose to depict them in his illustrations. L. Perry Curtis has drawn attention to Kavanagh's habit of bestowing hideous ape-like features on the Dublin police and British soldiers in his illustrations, with their 'huge mouths and bristling teeth' recalling the manner in which the London cartoonists

---

46 *The Irish Worker*, 27 September 1913. The fatalities referred to by Kavanagh and Clarke in their letters to Larkin's paper were James Nolan and John Byrne, two trade union members who lost their lives from injuries suffered at the hands of the police.

47 *Ibid.*, 6 September 1913.

48 *Ibid.*, 20 July 1912.

of the 1860s had earlier represented the Fenians of their day.[49]

Murphy was the recipient of equally ferocious treatment at the hands of Kavanagh's pen as the Dublin police. At various times Ireland's most eminent businessman was portrayed as a tyrant, thief and murderer in a series of notorious illustrations which became synonymous with *The Irish Worker* and its journalistic style. Labour historian Emmet O'Connor has observed that Murphy's enormous wealth and influence served James Larkin's 'compulsion to put a face on the enemy'.[50] The same is equally applicable with regards to Kavanagh, with Murphy replacing the stereotypically overweight and smug capitalist of his early labour cartoons as the Dublin Lockout became more and more personalised and bitterly fought. Although Kavanagh had depicted Murphy as a murderous scoundrel a full year before the outbreak of the Lockout, it was his cartoons attacking the leader of the Dublin Employers' Federation in the opening months of the great industrial dispute that gained him real notoriety.

Arnold Wright, in his employer-commissioned account of the Dublin Lockout published in 1914, invariably dismissed *The Irish Worker*'s representation of Murphy as a 'capitalistic ogre who battened on the sufferings of the poor and waxed rich on ill-gotten gains' as ludicrous.[51] Yet he was aware of the fact that not everyone shared his view, noting:

---

49 L. Perry Curtis, *Apes and Angels: The Irishman in Victorian caricature* (revised edition, Washington and London, 1997), p. 81. This artistic tactic becomes all the more striking when one considers the secret Fenian meetings which had been organised by Kavanagh's father at the family home during the 1860s – see p. 32 of this introduction.

50 O'Connor, *James Larkin*, p. 41.

51 Wright, *Disturbed Dublin*, p. 72.

The [*Irish Worker's*] Larkinite myth was too monstrous to excite in Dublin, where the facts are known, anything but ridicule. But it had its effect later, when the real clash of arms came and Mr Murphy stepped into the arena to conduct his historic fight with the sinister force which was strangling Dublin industry. Then certain English writers, as we shall have occasion to show, grasped eagerly at the idea presented to them by *The Irish Worker* … The impression then created has not been entirely obliterated.[52]

It is important to emphasise that it was not simply the endless barbed attacks in the columns of Larkin's paper that were responsible for Murphy's demonisation. For if these printed attacks in *The Irish Worker* were successful in swaying public opinion, they were still not nearly as effective, as Dermot Keogh has noted, as 'the savagely brilliant cartoons' of Kavanagh, which soon had many Dubliners referring to their city's foremost entrepreneur as William 'Murder' Murphy.[53] Nonetheless, save for Robert Lowery's one-sentence dismissal that while 'satirically clever' they 'lacked sophistication and were crudely drawn', existing studies of *The Irish Worker* have ignored Ernest Kavanagh's contribution to the paper.[54] It is clear from the context in which he made the statement that Lowery saw 'E.K.'s cartoons as one of *The Irish Worker's* 'defects'. Since Kavanagh's cartoons were likely one of the paper's most widely appreciated features, this suggestion is unfair. In an era where many workers had poor literacy levels and in which *The Irish Worker* faced fierce competition every week, the importance of his cartoons should not be underestimated. Considering that the paper

---

52 *Ibid.*, pp. 72–3.
53 Keogh, 'William Martin Murphy and the 1913 Dublin Lockout', p. 15.
54 Lowery, 'Sean O'Casey and *The Irish Worker*,' p. 45.

faced a never-ending battle against space restrictions and was dependent on advertising revenue for its very existence, the frequency and prominence of 'E.K.'s illustrations clearly reflects the level of importance in which Larkin and *The Irish Worker*'s readers held them.[55] With two-thirds appearing on the front page, they were an important method of getting people talking and attracting a new readership, and when one considers the style of the paper, it is clear that the lack of technical sophistication in 'E.K.'s cartoons should not be viewed negatively. If Kavanagh had produced more carefully drawn and 'sophisticated' cartoons they would have looked out of place in *The Irish Worker*, which essentially specialised in conveying messages of blunt immediacy.

This is not to discount their quality. Although always forcefully simple in their message, 'E.K.'s illustrations could sometimes be imbued with a range of subtleties in terms of their characterisation and attention to detail. Kavanagh's first contribution to *The Irish Worker* captures this complex simplicity perfectly, demonstrating the manner in which his cartoons complimented the rest of the paper's content and explaining why they would go on to become so synonymous with the publication. Unlike the paper's earlier artistic contributor, he recognised quite clearly that more could be achieved by satirising villains instead of glorifying heroes, a realisation that gave his work greater vitality and power. Furthermore, Kavanagh's harsh and almost childish strokes could imply an imbecility in his targets that captured *The Irish Worker*'s spirit by rendering them as utter objects of ridicule.

---

55   Pádraig Yeates, *Lockout: Dublin 1913* (Dublin 2000) p. 25.

'Shot dead by the British in a cold-blooded manner'?

Reading the description of his character by his friend Robert Monteith, it is easy to understand how Kavanagh had ended up working at Liberty Hall in a dual capacity:

> Poor E.K., an artist of promise whose art was ever at the service of his class and country without thought of reward … The poverty and wretchedness of the Dublin workers weighed heavily upon his heart, enshrouding him in pessimism when it did not half madden him. I have seen the blood surge in a crimson wave over his usually pale face at the sight of a shivering half-starved child whilst his hand went to his pocket for his last few coppers. It was not unusual for E.K. to dispose of his week's salary to the waifs and strays of Dublin within five hundred yards of Liberty Hall, where he was employed as a clerk in the Insurance Section of the Transport Workers' Union, leaving himself penniless for a week to come, and necessitating his walking to and from his home in Ranelagh.[56]

In the search for answers regarding the exact circumstances into Kavanagh's death, three separate accounts must be examined, two of which rely on second-hand information. A correspondent for *The Times*, who was in Dublin at the time of the Easter Rising, witnessed Kavanagh's shooting, and described what he had seen in a report promptly dispatched to the paper:

> We had gone only a little way when we were startled by the spectacle of a man shot dead on the steps of Liberty Hall, evidently the victim of a bullet from an invisible military rifle somewhere in the neighbourhood. The entrance to the Hall is commanded from the Custom House, and possibly a rifle shot from that quarter found its mark, as I subsequently learned that the man was a Sinn Féiner who had been either entering or leaving the Hall. Three or four women were quickly on the spot, raising the prostrate form

---

56   Robert Monteith, *Casement's Last Adventure* (Chicago 1932), pp. 6–7.

as we passed, and there was considerable excitement close by, although knowledge of the event had not at the time of our passing penetrated to the other side of the river, where crowds lined the streets in a state of anxious suspense.[57]

The rumour that Kavanagh was a 'Sinn Féiner' on account of his proximity to Liberty Hall was incorrect, and is indicative of how little most contemporary Dubliners understood the exact nature of the Rising while it was taking place. It needs also to be clarified that Kavanagh was seeking entry to Liberty Hall rather than leaving the building, which was empty at the time but for its caretaker, Peter Ennis, who later described what he had witnessed to Irish Citizen Army sergeant, Frank Robbins. Robbins was adamant that Ennis told him he had seen 'Ernest Kavanagh shot dead by the British in a cold-blooded manner', with the shots that 'blasted his life from this earth' coming from 'that portion of the Custom House facing the main entrance of Liberty Hall'.[58]

One thing that puzzled Robbins was Kavanagh's motive in going to Liberty Hall under such dangerous circumstances, since he knew that the cartoonist was not a member of the ICA and was not aware of him being an Irish Volunteer. Although Arthur Lynch was correct in stating to the House of Commons that Kavanagh had not been 'a member of any organisation which advocated physical force', his argument that he had simply approached Liberty Hall on Easter Tuesday to try to 'ascertain whether the staff was still there' can be disregarded.[59] The reality

---

57   *The [London] Times*, 29 April 1916.
58   Frank Robbins, BMH WS 585; Frank Robbins, *Under the Starry Plough. Recollections of the Irish Citizen Army* (Dublin 1977), pp. 239–40.
59   *Hansard, Vol. LXXXIV*, 13 July 1916.

is that Kavanagh, while unarmed and unjustly killed, was not simply some unfortunate innocent who was in the wrong place at the wrong time. His family were well informed about the planned Rising and he almost certainly visited Liberty Hall to offer his services as a rebel combatant. His sister Maeve (1878–1960) implied as much in a witness statement given to the Irish Defence Forces over three decades later:

> On Easter Tuesday morning Ernest went down town and went up the steps of Liberty Hall thinking some of the [Irish] Citizen Army might be there ... as he went up the steps he was killed – riddled with bullets fired by soldiers in the Custom House. He had told my sister that morning at breakfast that he could not sleep all night. He had not been a member of the [Irish] Volunteers or [Irish] Citizen Army.[60]

This supports the account given in the 1930s by Brian O'Neill, a labour journalist, that Kavanagh had 'set out for Liberty Hall to see if he could be of any help' to the ICA since, despite an admission to not knowing 'one end of a rifle from the other', he could 'bear inaction no longer'.[61] It appears likely that Kavanagh, suffering a guilty conscience for not joining the ICA's ranks and marching under James Connolly's command twenty-four hours earlier, was trying to make amends. Such a theory can be understood from comments made in a short obituary notice which was published in the *Catholic Bulletin* in December 1917. The journal stated that an 'inherent antipathy to discipline' had prevented Kavanagh from taking up a soldier's life, despite his 'active sympathy' with the rebels' cause.[62] It also noted that he 'was

---

60 Maeve Cavanagh MacDowell, BMH WS 258, p. 2.
61 *Irish Workers' Voice*, 16 July 1932.
62 *Catholic Bulletin*, December 1917, p. 781.

known to be absolutely fearless, and had a strange presentiment of his death', a fact confirmed by Robert Monteith fifteen years later, when he wrote that Kavanagh 'held the thought and the hope that his end would come swiftly'.[63]

In light of Liberty Hall's evacuation before the time that he was killed on its front steps, it seems probable that Kavanagh died at the hands of a military sniper stationed at the Custom House overlooking Beresford Place. Although the British government refused to pay any compensation following his death, the Kavanagh family were, at least, able to rely on Mortality Benefit payments from the ITGWU.[64] By 1916 both of Ernest's parents had passed away and this money would have been given to his eldest sister, Sarah Frazer (1862–1959), who was the head of the family household in Ranelagh at the time. The Kavanagh family was not wealthy but seem to have lived in relative comfort. Similar to their previous homes, the Oxford Road residence was always 'at the service of the nationalist cause'.[65] Ernest's father Michael, a Wexford-born clerk, had organised Fenian meetings at the family's Harold's Cross home in the build-up to the 1867 Rising, with James Stephens among the regular attendees.[66] A neighbour and friend, William Brophy, was one of the eight men selected by John Devoy in November 1865 to help rescue Stephens from Richmond Prison.[67] The physically imposing carpenter, who was married and had four children, was sentenced to fourteen years in

---

63 Monteith, *Casement's Last Adventure*, p. 6.
64 NLI, Ms 7,299, ITGWU Minute Book, 29 August & 3 September 1916. I would like to thank Francis Devine for alerting me to this information.
65 *Irish Press*, 6 March 1937.
66 *Ibid.*, 8 March 1937.
67 *Gaelic American*, 6 September 1913.

prison for his part in the successful rescue of the Fenian 'Chief'. This led Ernest's Dublin-born mother, Marianne (1845–95), taking great pity on Brophy, to regularly warn her husband against Stephens, whom she 'couldn't bear'. Sarah Frazer later recalled that her mother 'wasn't against the Fenians, only the man', and was often known to remark that 'Stephens, never fear, never got fourteen years'.[68]

Ernest's sister Maeve: 'the fair Poetess of the Revolution'

The Kavanagh children were firmly committed republicans like their father, with the likes of Countess Markievicz, Michael Mallin, Rory O'Connor and Frank Aiken later becoming regular visitors to the family home in Ranelagh. Ernest's sister Maeve, the third eldest daughter of the family, grew up idolising figures like Thomas Davis and Wolfe Tone, which led to her joining various branches of the Gaelic League during her early adulthood. Although she worked as a full-time milliner in Dublin for over forty years, it was as an artistic propagandist that she, like her brother, defined herself. In the opening decade of the twentieth century she began regularly contributing poems to W. P. Ryan's *Irish Peasant* and other nationalist newspapers, opting to spell her surname Cavanagh when not signing it in Irish (Maedb Caomanac). She also contributed poems to *The Irish Worker* on a regular basis. 'The Menace', published on 26 April 1913, arguably ranks as her most powerful labour poem from this period, vividly attacking society's elite for their inhumanity towards a hungry, bare-footed 'pallid boy' from the tenement slums:

---

68   *Irish Press*, 8 March 1937.

'Sell as ye have and give to the poor,'
We preach and we go our way.
Then why do you come with accusing gaze
At palace and stately homes we raise
And mock at the things we say?

Go back, pale boy, to your squalid world;
Nor stand like a menace there.
Is your lot too hard? Where the lush grass waves
In the paupers' ground o'er forgotten graves
There be room for your bones somewhere.[69]

Maeve also joined the Irish Citizen Army at this time, quickly becoming one of its most prominent female members. She had worked for a short time as a secretary for Cumann na mBan, a women's organisation which supported the Irish Volunteers, but left in frustration at how its members 'were only collecting money and such like activities'.[70] Although Maeve was happy to arrange fund-raisers for the ICA,[71] this decision was influenced by her ability to take part in 'all the activities' of the organisation, including attending military lectures at Liberty Hall, performing route marches across Dublin, as well as making frequent weekend trips to Countess Markievicz's cottage in the Dublin Mountains for target practice with revolvers and rifles.[72] Frank Robbins later claimed that her poem 'The Call To Arms', published in the *Workers' Republic* on 8 April 1916, captured perfectly 'the whole keynote of the mobilisation' carried out by the organisation in the weeks before the Rising, a mobilisation that left James Connolly

---

69 *The Irish Worker*, 26 April 1913.
70 Maeve Cavanagh MacDowell, BMH WS 258, p. 3.
71 *Workers' Republic*, 8 April 1916.
72 Maeve Cavanagh MacDowell, BMH WS 258, p. 3.; *Irish Press*, 18 April 1938.

and Michael Mallin (the general-commandant and chief of staff) 'exultant and proud'.[73] In the poem Maeve shows herself to be full of admiration for the Irishmen rushing to Liberty Hall at the end of a hard day's work to fight for their country's freedom:

> Make way, oh gaping, careless crowds,
> Fall back, and let them by
> Fate even now may weave their shrouds,
> They go – to win or die.
> Some moments since, at work they bent,
> In factory, mill or street,
> Till Eire, her Reveille sent,
> Then thronged they to her feet.
>
> Machines were stay'd, tools thrown aside,
> 'Twas Eire's hosting day,
> Ne'er bridegroom to a regal bride,
> Went half so fleet as they.
> With bandolier and trusty gun,
> Each busy street they tread,
> Whilst England's craven garrison,
> Looks on in hate, and dread.[74]

Cavanagh's admiration for the Dublin workers of 1913 who 'walked rather than ride in the blackleg trams ... starved rather than give in', was no doubt strongly felt.[75] However, it is clear that the issue of national freedom was always her main priority and she evidently shared James Connolly's view that, until English rule was ended in Ireland, 'the social revolution would never come'.[76] Connolly became a trusted friend of Cavanagh's, and she

73 Robbins, *Under the Starry Plough*, p. 60.
74 *Workers' Republic*, 8 April 1916.
75 Fox, *Rebel Irishwomen*, p. 156.
76 Maeve Cavanagh MacDowell, BMH WS 258, p. 7.

greatly admired his ability to 'attract a better type of man' than the more popular Larkin.[77] The admiration was mutual: Connolly 'quickly saw the value of Maeve Cavanagh's poems in feeding the revolutionary flame', regularly printing them on the front page of *The Irish Worker* (during his editorship of the paper in its final months) and the *Workers' Republic* (which he had re-launched and edited in the eleven months before his death).[78] He also ensured Maeve's lasting fame by publicly labelling her 'the fair poetess of the Revolution' in December 1915,[79] some eight years after he had written that 'no revolutionary movement is complete without its poetical expression'.[80]

When one considers her opinion of Connolly it is easy to see why such praise and respect for her poetic role left Maeve feeling 'very proud'.[81] In her poem 'Leaderless', published in *The Irish Worker* on 10 August 1912, she had yearned for a strong heroic figure to come to Ireland's rescue:

> When shall rise a Leader
> Such as Eire knew
> When Tone held high in his strong hands
> The Torch that all might view?
>
> Come, forth, oh, Leader,
> A scattered army we,
> Irresolute, with flickering lights,
> We stand awaiting thee.[82]

---

77   *Ibid.*, p. 4.
78   Fox, *Rebel Irishwomen*, p. 157.
79   *Workers' Republic*, 11 December 1915.
80   Connolly made this comment in his introduction to *Songs of Freedom*, published in New York in 1907. See Donal Nevin (ed.), *Writings of James Connolly. Collected Works* (Dublin 2011), p. 39.
81   Maeve Cavanagh MacDowell, BMH WS 258, p. 6.
82   *Irish Worker*, 10 August 1912.

Following the Easter Rising she made it clear that one man had valiantly answered her call. In 'James Connolly, I.R.A.', the opening poem from her hastily produced collection *A Voice of Insurgency*, she wrote:

> Profoundly Ireland mourns today
> Her Leader wise whom God had sent,
> Who sleeps in blood-soaked prison clay,
> Yet sorrow is with Triumph blent,
> For thro' the land his spirit goes,
> And Freedom's seed still deeper sows.[83]

In Maeve Cavanagh's mind Connolly was her generation's answer to Wolfe Tone, a titan of a man who showed the courage and ability to lead Ireland into battle with England as others, such as Bulmer Hobson and Eoin MacNeill, disgraced their country by continuing to hesitate and adopting a defensive strategy. One Cavanagh poem, 'Ireland to Germany', was quoted in the House of Commons as evidence of an Irish–German plot against Britain, and there is no doubt that she was considered a dangerous propagandist by the British authorities. The poem had initially been intended for publication in Connolly's *Workers' Republic* but was censored by Dublin Castle. Connolly later mocked this decision and described Cavanagh's poem as 'a piece of verse calculated to make the red blood hot in the veins of every true lover of freedom in Ireland'.[84] Reading it one can see why the British authorities had been so alarmed by the poem's content and were eager for it not to enter the public domain:

---

83   Maeve Cavanagh, *A Voice of Insurgency* (Dublin 1916), p. 13.
84   *Workers' Republic*, 11 December 1915.

> Thy stroke be sure, oh, Germany,
> This wish I send you o'er the sea,
> From Shannon fair to lordly Rhine,
> The foe who fronts thee, too, is mine;
> Could'st be, my hosts with thine would be,
> And my revenge – thy victory.
>
> My sons, as thine, are true and brave,
> To aid thee in thy task they crave,
> To bring the pride of England low
> And vengeance wreak for all my woe,
> God grant 'tis thine to overthrow
> And crush to earth our common foe.[85]

Another poem to appear in *A Voice of Insurgency*, 'Ireland's overture to Germany', featured similarly inflammatory anti-British sentiments:

> Proud Germany, if thou had'st been
> The fiercest nation earth had seen,
> With no one thing to choose between
> Your sins and hers,
>
> I'd still to thee my hand extend,
> Thy hate and mine for her should blend
> For e'er her foe shall be my friend
> Her friend my foe.[86]

An admirer of her pre-1916 poems later claimed that they played a key role in encouraging the revolutionary spirit of Irish rebels at the time: 'on reading them, strong men and true women, already straining at the leash which held them back, were even more anxious for the fray'.[87]

---

85   Cavanagh, *A Voice of Insurgency*, p. 43.
86   *Ibid.*, p. 48.
87   Quote taken from Fox, *Rebel Irishwomen*, pp. 153–4.

Yet Maeve Cavanagh was no mere cheerleader in 1916. As a member of the Irish Citizen Army she was also a participant, acting as one of James Connolly's dispatch messengers on Easter Monday. The day before, just hours after Eoin MacNeill had sought to scupper the Rising by dramatically issuing a counter-manding order against all planned Irish Volunteer manoeuvres later that day, she had attended a concert in Liberty Hall. As the night came to a close Maeve met with Connolly for the last time. Under the watchful eye of a Dublin policeman beneath 'the gloomy arches of Beresford Place' just metres away, he informed her 'with a grim and determined air' that the Rising was to go ahead the following day despite the recent setbacks and confusion.[88] He then asked her to return to Liberty Hall at eight o'clock the next morning to receive her dispatch order, laughing at Maeve's surprised reaction and the notion that this time could be considered 'too early for the Irish Revolution' to take place.[89]

It transpired that Maeve did not have to return to Liberty Hall. During the night a sealed envelope was delivered to her house for her to bring to Waterford.[90] The following morning she went there by train and informed Seán Matthews, the local Irish Volunteer officer, of Connolly's determination to 'fight at noon'.[91] Matthews was clearly troubled by the news, revealing that he had earlier received a conflicting order to demobilise his men from Captain J. J. O'Connell, who had since travelled to Kilkenny to issue the same message.[92] Maeve agreed to follow

---

88 Fox, *Rebel Irishwomen*, p. 158.
89 Maeve Cavanagh MacDowell, BMH WS 258, pp. 9–10.
90 *Ibid.*, p. 10.
91 Fox, *Rebel Irishwomen*, p. 159.
92 Maeve Cavanagh MacDowell, BMH WS 258, p. 10.

O'Connell to Kilkenny hoping that he could be persuaded to call off demobilisation and allow the Waterford and Kilkenny Volunteers to take 'combined action' in the Rising.[93] To Cavanagh's consternation, however, O'Connell broke down in tears when she later spoke with him, convinced from reading the latest edition of an English newspaper that the Rising was already doomed.[94] She returned to Waterford with his message that 'nothing could be done, the thing was practically over'.[95]

Eager to return home from what had clearly become a fool's errand and take part 'in the Rising', Maeve was forced to wait until Saturday before the next train to Dublin was available.[96] After a 'very tedious and slow journey' she finally arrived home in Ranelagh later that day, where, upon opening the door, her teenage nephew bluntly informed her that 'Ernest is killed'.[97] Since Ernest Kavanagh was not a member of the Irish Citizen Army or Irish Volunteers, this news came as an enormous shock to Maeve. It was Willie Kavanagh, another brother who had recently returned home from England and also carried a dispatch message for Connolly on Easter Monday, who would have been more at risk in her mind.[98]

Maeve's devastation at the news of Ernest's death was immense. Her attachment to him and numbness at his loss was poignantly revealed in the opening verses of a tribute poem which appeared in *A Voice of Insurgency* eight months after his death:

---

93   *Ibid.*
94   *Ibid.*, p. 12.
95   *Ibid.*
96   *Ibid.*, p. 10.
97   *Ibid.*, p. 13. Maeve's nephew was Ernest Frazer (1900–1959), who lived with the Kavanagh family in Ranelagh along with his mother Sarah.
98   *Ibid.*, pp. 8–9.

When first they told me you were dead,
I scarcely felt Grief's pain,
Straight in the face I looked black Dread,
And barred it from my brain.

I shed no tears, I turned to hear
Your step at every sound,
So strong your presence seemed and near
That Wonder sorrow drowned.

How strange it seemed, I saw a draft,
Your hand had just laid there,
And all the small things of your craft
Beside your empty chair.

Brother and sister were we two
Comrades, soul-friends beside,
And yet how dear I hardly knew
Till now when you have died …[99]

Not surprisingly *A Voice of Insurgency* proved hugely popular with Irish nationalists, selling out within a matter of weeks. Maeve continued to prolifically churn out further volumes of nationalist poems, with *Soul and Clay* published shortly after the second edition of *A Voice of Insurgency* in 1917. The next year she succeeded in publishing *Passion Flowers*, her fourth collection of verse, which 'had to be printed at night' for fear of raids by the 'military literati'.[100] One of its most powerful poems, 'In Brave '16', mocked 'barbarous England' for their harsh and counterproductive approach to dealing with the Rising:

And when she thought the last lay dead
She breathed free again.

---

99 Cavanagh, *A Voice of Insurgency*, pp. 22–3.
100 *Idem, Soul and Clay* (Dublin 1917), p. 3.

> She saw not in her blinded hate
> The worth of martyr blood
> Where erst some hundred rebels were
> Now vengeful thousands stood.[101]

Although it is clear that Maeve Cavanagh had many admirers, it is rather easy to dismiss her work. After all, she herself was self-deprecating about the quality of her poems, once describing them as 'unfinished, rude ... scant of beauty ... and crude' verse that was merely designed to reflect national feeling and aimed for a readership whose souls were 'simple'.[102] In the preface to *Soul and Clay* F. R. Higgins stressed his belief that her poetry should not be judged artistically by 'lofty' critics, but instead simply recognised as the powerful songs 'for the Irish democracy' that they were.[103] Historian R. M. Fox later echoed this notion that Cavanagh's poems did not belong to 'the "Art for Art's sake" school'.[104] He praised Maeve's bravery in attaching her poetry 'to the chariot of life', feeling that her post-Rising poems reflected the changing 'national mood and spirit' in Ireland at the time and showed the Dublin poetess at her 'resolute and sure' best.[105]

Cathal MacDowell and *Cartoons. Ernest Kavanagh ('E.K.') of 'The Worker'*

An important figure had emerged in Maeve's life by this time. Whereas before the Easter Rising she had often 'worked side by side' with her brother, after 1916 she had a new partner to

---

101 *Idem., Passion Flowers* (Dublin 1918), p. 24.
102 *Idem., A Voice of Insurgency*, p. 12.
103 *Idem., Soul and Clay*, p. 4.
104 Fox, *Rebel Irishwomen*, p. 153.
105 *Ibid.*, pp. 153, 163.

collaborate with. This was Cathal MacDowell, an engineer for Dublin Corporation, who had fought with the Irish Volunteers during 1916 and who Maeve eventually married on 26 April 1921. At the time of the Rising, however, the pair did not know one another. MacDowell discovered his future wife having heard her poems read aloud by other rebel prisoners during his incarceration at Richmond Barracks and Frongoch Prison Camp, an experience which led him to seek an introduction upon his release shortly afterwards.[106] In addition to becoming romantically linked, Maeve and Cathal went on to work together professionally over the coming years, sharing 'dreams, and hopes, and quests'.[107] MacDowell was a talented composer and the couple collaborated to write a series of satirical nationalist ballads during the Anglo-Irish War.[108] The *Irish Press* newspaper later recorded that these songs poked 'devastating fun at the enemy' and were recited 'at every rebel gathering' of the time.[109] These ballads were particularly effective during the 1918 general election, with songs such as 'We'll crown de Valera King of Ireland' proving popular with many Dublin street children and helping Sinn Féin's candidates to wrest political power from John Redmond's Irish Parliamentary Party.[110]

It was at this time that Maeve and Cathal also published a small booklet of Ernest Kavanagh's cartoons at the behest of Countess Markievicz. Upon hearing of the Dublin cartoonist's death in 1916, the imprisoned Markievicz was determined to

---

106 Maeve Cavanagh MacDowell, BMH WS 258, p. 1.
107 NLI, Maeve Cavanagh MacDowell Papers, Ms 21,562.
108 *Ibid.*
109 *Irish Press*, 7 March 1934.
110 *Ibid.*

ensure that steps to preserve his legacy were taken, writing in a letter to her sister:

> I was so sorry to hear about Ernest. He was a bit of a genius. Will try and write something. Tell Maev [*sic*] to collect his drawings, original and reproductions. We'll bring them out some day.[111]

This plan was hindered by the seizure of all Kavanagh's original non-political sketches in the aftermath of the Easter Rising during one of several military raids carried out on his former home.[112] Furthermore, when *Cartoons. Ernest Kavanagh ('E.K.') of 'The Worker'* was finally ready for publication in early 1918, Markievicz was still imprisoned in England. As a result it was Cathal MacDowell who wrote the introduction to the booklet, during which he expressed his hope that the family friend would soon be at liberty and thus 'fulfil her kind promise as to the introductory matter' when the other three planned volumes of Kavanagh's cartoons were collected and published in the future.[113] With his close family connection and own ability as a 'clever artist' (specialising in the architectural sphere) MacDowell was an obvious choice to replace Markievicz in introducing 'E.K.'s work.[114] He wrote:

> Ernest Kavanagh was a keen student of human nature ... men that he deemed hypocrites, cowards, tyrants, or liars, these he minutely

---

111 Jacqueline Van Voris, *Constance de Markievicz: in the cause of Ireland* (Amherst 1967), p. 266. Markievicz's sister, Eva Gore-Booth, had possibly learned of Ernest's death while campaigning for Roger Casement with Maeve in early August 1916. See Maeve Cavanagh MacDowell, BMH WS 258, pp. 15–16; NLI, Maeve Cavanagh MacDowell Papers, Ms 21,561.

112 Cavanagh, *A Voice of Insurgency* (second edition, Dublin 1917), p. 8.

113 *Cartoons. Ernest Kavanagh ('E.K.') of 'The Worker'* (Dublin 1918), p. 1.

114 *Irish Press*, 7 March 1934.

dissected … His technique may not be perfect, but his message in each case is clearly and forcibly told … [He] used his talents without any remuneration to raise the ideals of others to the level of his own … [He was] a most talented and thoughtful artist.[115]

While a good introduction to Kavanagh's work, and invaluable in that almost half of the twenty illustrations it contained were either unpublished or appeared on contemporary postcards that are now lost, the booklet nonetheless fails to do him justice. Many of his most vivid and memorable surviving pieces are missing and, in light of the failure to publish the other three planned editions of his illustrations, it is to the pages of *The Irish Worker* and other newspapers from the time that we are best advised to turn today to gain a greater appreciation of his artistic efforts to free Ireland from what he perceived as the scourges of social inequality, capitalism and British occupancy.

Ernest Kavanagh's suffrage and anti-recruitment/nationalist cartoons

A handful of powerful 'E.K.' cartoons were published in the *Irish Citizen*, a weekly Dublin-based newspaper of the women's suffrage movement which had been set up by Francis Sheehy-Skeffington and James Cousins on 25 May 1912. The paper's masthead motto – *For Men and Women Equally the Rights of Citizenship; From Men and Women Equally the Duties of Citizenship* – demonstrated the editorial policy of the *Irish Citizen*, with the issue of 'Votes for Women' invariably dominating the paper's pages throughout its opening years. During this time the *Irish Citizen* supported the introduction of Home Rule on principle, though repeatedly

---

115 *Cartoons. Ernest Kavanagh*, pp. 1–2.

emphasised that it would amount to little more than 'Male Rule' unless women were enfranchised before a bill of Irish self-determination had been passed.[116] This view was supported by Ernest Kavanagh, whose cartoons for the paper attacked the unjustness and hypocrisy of Irish men regarding their attitudes towards women. Although the editors of the *Irish Citizen* viewed Will Dyson, the pro-suffrage cartoonist of the *Daily Herald*, as 'easily the greatest cartoonist now working in these islands',[117] upon publication of Kavanagh's famous first cartoon for the paper, 'The Angel of Freedom', they praised him as a young artist with the 'promise of a brilliant future'.[118] This cartoon became a powerful propaganda image for the women's suffrage movement in Ireland, causing John Redmond and the Irish Parliamentary Party, whom it negatively depicted, considerable embarrassment.

Redmond also came in for scathing treatment from Kavanagh in his anti-recruitment cartoons for *The Irish Worker* during the paper's final months, the majority of which were accompanied by equally savage poems from his sister. As Ben Novick has pointed out, *The Irish Worker* 'detested the war and wished for Ireland to remain neutral, in alliance with working men around the world'.[119] Kavanagh's artistic skill became a key weapon of the paper during the opening months of the war, especially during James Connolly's editorship in its final months, when his cartoons presented 'a caricatured chronology of Redmond's

116 See Louise Ryan, 'The *Irish Citizen*, 1912–1920', *Saothar* 17 (1992), p. 107.

117 *Irish Citizen*, 5 April 1913.

118 *Ibid.*, 15 March 1913.

119 Ben Novick, *Conceiving Revolution: Irish Nationalist Propaganda during the First World War* (Dublin 2001), pp. 192–3.

recruiting efforts'.[120] These 'biting cartoons', as later described by Sean O'Casey in his short history of the Irish Citizen Army, were fiercely critical of the notion of Irish Volunteers fighting for Britain in the First World War.[121]

As the war progressed Ernest Kavanagh shared his sister's disdain for Bulmer Hobson and Eoin MacNeill, viewing them both as 'bluffers' rather than fighters who possessed the courage necessary to take advantage of England's difficulty and lead a rebellion.[122] In a lost cartoon he depicted both men at a committee meeting of the Irish Volunteers which had been ambushed by James Larkin, making them look 'very frightened' and seen to demand Larkin's expulsion as 'a "real" revolutionary'.[123] Kavanagh was a good friend of Larkin's and does not seem to have judged him harshly for leaving Ireland in 1914 when, to use his sister's words, 'the Revolution was coming off'.[124]

'The Artist of the Revolution'

In his introduction to *Cartoons. Ernest Kavanagh ('E.K.') of 'The Worker'* Cathal MacDowell admitted that his brother-in-law's cartoons did not represent mainstream Irish opinion at the time:

> Many of those whom Ernest Kavanagh lauded were despised when he depicted them, most of those whom he despised were respected then. But times have changed, and opinions with them. In many of his pictures he was prophetic. I do not wish to single out any particular names as examples of his judgment of aim and character:

---

120 *Ibid.*, p. 193.
121 Sean O'Casey, *The Story of the Irish Citizen Army* (London, Journeyman Press Edition, 1980), p. 44.
122 *Cartoons. Ernest Kavanagh*, p. 1.
123 *Ibid.*
124 Maeve Cavanagh MacDowell, BMH WS 258, p. 4.

he was at variance with Irish public opinion when he drew; readers can judge for themselves who was right – Ernest Kavanagh or the Irish public.[125]

By 1918, when MacDowell made his statement, Ireland had undergone a tremendous amount of change and the traumatic events of the previous few years had led to a definite shift in public opinion towards both the country's leading employers and the issue of Home Rule.

An examination of some cartoons featured in the Dublin-based *Lepracaun* journal offers a revealing insight into Irish public opinion at the time that Kavanagh drew. Thomas Fitzpatrick, a greatly admired Irish cartoonist, had set up this popular cartoon monthly in May 1905. In the journal's early years 'Fitz' contributed many of the cartoons himself, attacking 'everything appertaining to cant, sham, and humbug'.[126] However, by 1911 his health had deteriorated rapidly – he passed away the following summer – and the *Lepracaun* came to rely on 'Spex' (John Fergus O'Hea) and 'S.H.Y.' (an unknown Dublin cartoonist) to fill its pages. The cartoons of these two artists over the next several years offer a striking comparison and contrast to Kavanagh's labour illustrations. On the one hand, O'Hea was happy to lambast the baton-wielding Dublin police for their attacks on striking workers and their families. In two cartoons almost identical to Kavanagh's *Irish Worker* representations, the DMP were criticised for their indiscriminate batoning of 'ord'nary citizens' and how they 'ran "amok" in the City of Dublin' in late August 1913.[127] Yet as the Dublin Lockout progressed, O'Hea was keen to emphasise that

---

125 *Cartoons. Ernest Kavanagh*, p. 1.

126 *The Lepracaun*, July 1912.

127 *Ibid.*, September 1911 & October 1913.

it was the same 'ord'nary citizens' (i.e. non-trade unionists) who were the real victims of the epic struggle and were 'getting the worst of it'.[128] 'S.H.Y.' also attacked Larkin as an untrustworthy and destructive 'strike monger' in two separate 1913 cartoons.[129]

Mention of the *Lepracaun* leads us to the suggestion that Ernest Kavanagh's cartoons were perhaps too bitter in nature. For although some 'E.K.' illustrations showed definite glimpses of humour, by and large Kavanagh's work was characterised by an anger and indignation which set him apart from his fellow artists. For example, the *Lepracaun*'s obituary notice for Thomas Fitzpatrick contained the following anecdote:

> On one occasion, having caricatured a prominent politician of his acquaintance somewhat severely, he was unexpectedly accosted by the subject who, producing a copy of the paper, demanded indignantly – 'What the divil did you do that for?' whereupon 'Fitz', with a twinkle in his grey-blue eye, responded – 'What the divil did you deserve it for?' And then – the spectacle of cartoonist and cartooned marching off together arm-in-arm the best of friends.[130]

Another Irish cartoonist of considerable reputation, Charles Edward Kelly, later spent over four decades contributing satirical illustrations to the pages of the popular *Dublin Opinion* magazine which he co-edited. His daughter, journalist Pauline Bracken, recalled how originals of the cartoons by 'C.E.K.' and the other *Dublin Opinion* contributors were 'often asked for' by the subjects they targeted.[131] Such outcomes with regard to Kavanagh and the individuals whom he specifically targeted in his cartoons are

---

128 *Ibid.*, November 1913.
129 *Ibid.*, August 1913 & Christmas Number 1913.
130 *Ibid.*, July 1912.
131 Pauline Bracken, *Light of Other Days. A Dublin Childhood* (Cork 1992), p. 31.

impossible to imagine, since it was his trademark to vilify them in seeking to rouse the conscience of the Irish public rather than trying to raise laughs at their expense.

James Larkin would not have wanted it any other way. When he had launched *The Irish Worker* in May 1911 the ITGWU general secretary was no doubt hoping to replicate the success and impact of the English-based *Daily Herald*, a rebellious socialist paper which had been founded just a few months earlier and was sold at Liberty Hall. One of the *Daily Herald*'s most notable weapons was its ferocious cartoons by Will Dyson. Like Kavanagh, Dyson's cartoons furiously championed militancy in the labour movement and there is no doubt that Larkin was keen for Kavanagh to serve his paper in the same way. In its first year of circulation *The Irish Worker* published over a dozen cartoons by 'C.B.', yet this series varied in power and tended to merely take jabs at its targets rather than seeking to land any knockout blows.[132] Kavanagh's illustrations proved to have far more impact and this probably played a key role in ensuring that he became *The Irish Worker*'s new cartoonist in 1912.

It took him over a year to discover the artistic talent of Ernest Kavanagh but, when he did, Larkin had found an artist who could perfectly compliment the potent written word of his paper. 'E.K.' was undoubtedly *The Irish Worker*'s ideal cartoonist. While it is true his work possesses more historical importance than artistic merit, his talent is unquestionable. Kavanagh may not have been as technically accomplished or politically incisive as other more celebrated cartoonists from his era, yet his illustrations could

---

132 The identity of 'C.B.' is unknown, but we know from a signature attached to one cartoon that the artist's surname was Byrne. See *The Irish Worker*, 23 December 1911.

nearly always be relied upon to serve their purpose and provoke a reaction. He possessed the classic cartoonist skill of being able to exaggerate the facial and bodily features of his targets without disguising their identity, and the best of his distorted depictions of Redmond, Murphy and the Dublin police have left us with defining images of the multifaceted protests in Ireland during the years leading up to 1916. Whether one agrees that he should be described as 'The Artist of the Revolution', a moniker allegedly coined by James Connolly,[133] it is clear that Ernest Kavanagh deserves to be remembered for devoting his energies and artistic talent to 'the national and kindred movements, more particularly the cause of Labour' during his tragically short life.[134]

---

133 *Irish Press*, 18 April 1938. In an article about Maeve Cavanagh's visit to the cottage formerly owned by Countess Markievicz in the Dublin mountains, which she had frequented often, it was stated that '[James] Connolly called Maeve Cavanagh MacDowell the poet of the revolution, and her brother Ernest, who was killed in Easter Week, the artist of the revolution'. No other record of this description of Ernest Kavanagh exists, yet it seems plausible that such a comment was made by Connolly, especially in private, following his declaration in the *Workers' Republic* that Maeve was Ireland's 'fair poetess of the Revolution'.

134 *Catholic Bulletin*, December 1917, p. 781.

The Labour Cartoons

This cartoon, published on 6 July 1912, was Ernest Kavanagh's first to appear in *The Irish Worker*. Although blunt in its message the cartoon possesses great subtlety. As the sweat from the labourer's brow drips downwards, the smoke from the employer's cigar billows upwards. As the labourer almost imperceptibly glances up from his bent-over position, the employer stands upright and peers down. The labourer's pulled-up sleeves clearly reveal a muscular physique, in stark contrast to the employer's concealed yet obviously bloated figure. Together with the cartoon's caption, the underlying suggestion behind all of these contrasts is that the abused worker should ignore the mainstream press and, quite literally, stand up for his rights. He should realise that he and his fellow labourers possessed the power to topple complacent employers and rectify all of their industrial grievances. This notion echoes James Larkin's dismissal of the mainstream press and call for Ireland's labouring class to symbolically 'forge their weapons and fight' in the first issue of *The Irish Worker*.[1]

---

1   *The Irish Worker*, 27 May 1911.

The employers' and the workers' interests are identical (Daily Paper)
(We don't think !)

All images in this book are reproduced courtesy of the National Library of Ireland

'WORKER AND SWEATER'

Published on 20 July 1912, this was Ernest Kavanagh's second cartoon to appear in *The Irish Worker*. It again urges the workers of Ireland to unite and fight, in this instance for a fair living wage from bosses who had grown rich on money 'sweated from the worker'. It also attacks the Dublin police and British military for proving themselves to be part of 'the capitalist State apparatus of suppression of the workers', to borrow a phrase from a later labour journalist commenting on Kavanagh's cartoons, and protecting tyrannical Irish employers from receiving their comeuppance.[2]

The cartoon accompanied an anonymous poem, from which the following extract is taken:

> 'If your union tries to "back" you
> Then, by heaven, I will sack you!'
> Says the dear kind boss as on his swag he sits;
> 'My police will make you move on,
> But their bludgeons I'll improve on
> By getting out my soldiers to blow you into bits.'
>
> Then the worker fairly cowed,
> Almost begs to be allowed
> To keep his job at the old sweated rate;
> And the boss laughs up his sleeve,
> He has good cause to believe
> That his robbery is winked at by the State.

---

2   *Irish Workers' Voice*, 16 July 1932.

'A GRAFTON STREET IDYLL'

This cartoon was published in *The Irish Worker* on 3 August 1912, accompanying a comic poem by 'Mac' (A. P. Wilson), which ridiculed the typical frequenters of Dublin's main shopping thoroughfare:

> Oh, there's only one possible place to go
> If you just want to see Dublin's fashion show,
> If you want to be fast and not to be slow
> Try Grafton street, it cannot be beat.
>
> From the Bishop in gaiters and smile so sweet,
> To the Johnny whose brains are all on his feet,
> And the girls who for foolishness can't be beat,
> They're found complete in Grafton street.

The Irish Worker regularly mocked Irish men and women who aped

foreign fashions, arguing that they only succeeded in making themselves look ridiculous while neglecting home-grown manufacturers.

'THE GUARDIAN OF
THE PACE'[3]

Published in *The Irish
Worker* on 10 August
1912, this cartoon glo-
rifies the fighting spirit
of Ireland's working
class population and at-
tacks their treatment at
the hands of the Dub-
lin police. It depicts
a plucky and defiant
old woman refusing to
budge when confront-
ed by a towering Dub-
lin policeman who, upon observing her selling apples on a street
corner, orders the woman home if she wishes to avoid a charge of
public obstruction. The implication is that the DMP were more in-
terested in flexing their muscles and persecuting the poor on trivial
charges than tackling serious crimes.

The cartoon accompanied a poem by 'Mac' (A. P. Wilson), from
which the following extract is taken:

> 'I'll not stir a step, neither me nor me fruit,
> For yersilf, Mr. Polisman, ye ugly ould brute!'
> 'Just moind what yer sayin'!' roared the man in blue.
> 'Oh, I moind what I'm sayin', but I won't stir for you.
> It's not me nor me apples that's obstructing the street,
> But yerself, Mr. Polisman, yerself an' yer feet!'

---

3   'Pace' was how many Dubliners pronounced 'peace' during Kavanagh's
    lifetime.

'A Dublin Slum House'

This cartoon was published in *The Irish Worker* on 24 August 1912, alongside another Kavanagh cartoon depicting a labourer at a public house buying a pint of stout. James Larkin was sickened by the amount of time and money most workers spent in public houses at the end of their working week. This led him to set up the weekly Liberty Hall family concerts each Sunday, events at which it was customary for Maeve Cavanagh to play the piano. Ernest Kavanagh's sister was equally disgusted by the problem of drunkenness in Ireland. In a letter to *The Irish Worker*, published on 5 October 1912, she attacked the problem of 'beastial gluttony' and captured the key message of her brother's cartoon by declaring how 'one's whole sympathy goes out to the inmates of the homes that await these specimens of the publicans' greed'.[4]

The cartoon accompanied a poem by 'Mac' (A. P. Wilson), from which the following extract is taken:

> See where the worker passeth his time!
> Wasting his time, his manhood and health;
> Giving his earnings to swell that wealth
> Which from the poor and needy is wrung
> By the soulless ghouls who deal in bung.
> The ghouls who shatter his whole home life;
> The fiends who murder his children and wife.

---

4   *The Irish Worker*, 5 October 1912.

'THE HASS AND 'ORSE SHOW'

Mocking a high-profile gala event at the RDS stadium in Ballsbridge which was taking place that same day, this cartoon appeared in the 31 August 1912 issue of *The Irish Worker*. Horse Show Week was an annual tradition dating back to 1864, which saw the aristocracy of Ireland and abroad flood into Dublin for a few days each summer to enjoy what *The Irish Times* proudly called 'the greatest horse show in the world'.[5] Unsurprisingly *The Irish Worker* was consistently hostile to the event. In 1911 James Larkin went undercover at the RDS during Horse Show Week disguised as a labourer, an experience that led him to pen an article lambasting the 'starvation' wages and 'tyrannous treatment' which he witnessed as 'nothing short of a public scandal'.[6] Alongside Kavanagh's cartoon in August 1912 appeared another critical article. An anonymous writer was indignant at how 'thousands of pounds' were spent each year feeding animals, the best of which were then invariably sold abroad to the detriment of Irish cattle farming, while people died of starvation across Dublin and 'hungry schoolchildren' were forced to go without dinners.[7] Kavanagh's cartoon is set on Grafton Street, Dublin's famous shopping thoroughfare, and mocks the snobbish women with upturned noses and foolish 'Johnnies' who frequented expensive shops such as Switzers (now Brown Thomas) during Horse Show Week, all the while lapping up the lies, sensationalism and anti-Home Rule hysteria regularly printed in the mainstream press.

The cartoon accompanied a memorable comic poem by 'Mac' (A. P. Wilson), from which the following extracts are taken:

---

5   *The Irish Times*, 25 August 1913.
6   *The Irish Worker*, 26 August 1911.
7   *Ibid.*, 31 August 1912.

'Tis out at Ballsbridge that the horses are seen.
And of finer gee-gees you couldn't well dream.
'Tis in Grafton street that the donkeys parade
And sillier asses can't be found, I'm afraid …

No, nothing is new, 'tis the same old tale
That is told every year after year without fail
The horses are shown for the asses to view
And the nags have by far the most sense of the two.

'Our Lord Mayor'

This cartoon appeared in *The Irish Worker* on 7 September 1912, ridiculing the then holder of the mayoral office of Dublin, Lorcan G. Sherlock. Sherlock was a frequent target for ridicule in *The Irish Worker* and regularly appeared in Kavanagh's cartoons for the paper, albeit usually in a supporting role. Although he was actually quite popular during his time as Lord Mayor of Dublin, *The Irish Worker* saw him as a man both small in stature and achievements: a 'pocket Napoleon' who was vain, vastly overpaid, hypocritical, and full of promises which he never kept.[8] The paper attacked the gross unjustness of Sherlock earning a huge annual salary while the Mountjoy Ward constituency which he represented was home to slums that were 'hot-beds of filth and fever, spawning beds of vice and crime; without sanitation; without light; yet open to the elements – to rain and cold'.[9] While the Lord Mayor may have earned praise for his habit of making loud speeches about necessary reforms, Kavanagh's cartoon and an accompanying poem by 'Oscar' conveyed *The Irish Worker*'s view that these performances were simply not taken seriously by anybody who listened.

---

8   *The Irish Worker*, 21 October 1911.
9   *Ibid.*

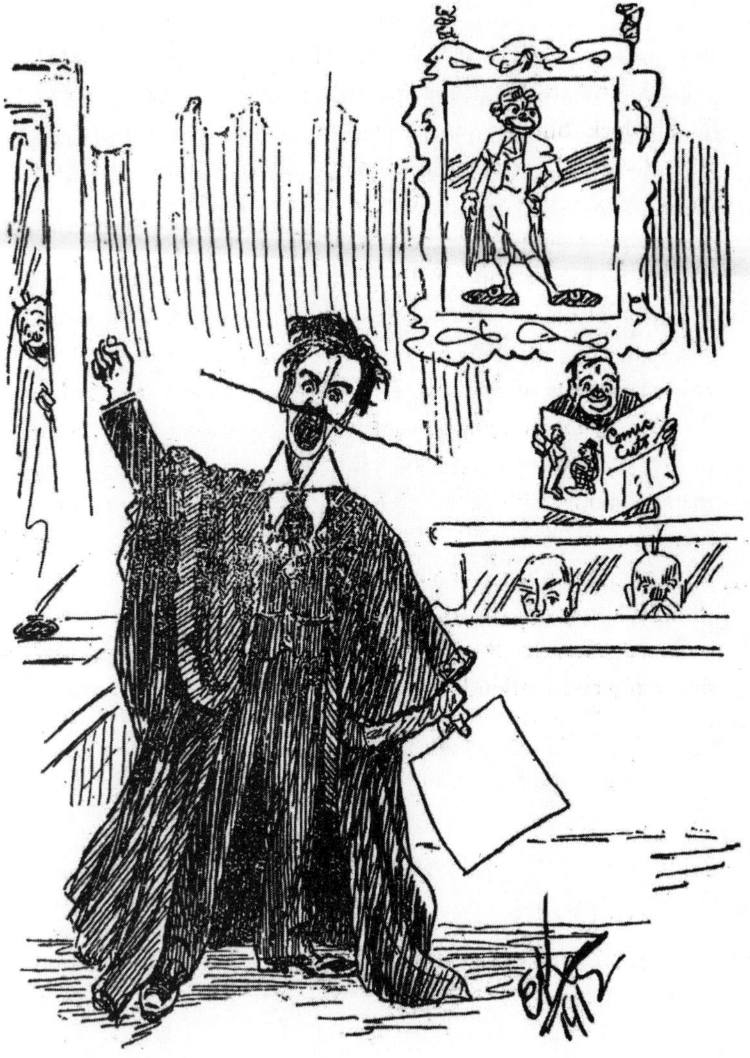
Comic Cuts

'THE ASSININE LAW'

Published in *The Irish Worker* on 14 September 1912, this cartoon attacks the unjust nature of the Irish legal system. It depicts a donkey, dressed as a judge, dishing out 'Law by the Classes for the Masses'. Kavanagh's illustration accompanied a comic poem by 'Mac' (A. P. Wilson), from which the following extracts are taken:

> It's the Classes who furnish the Law,
> Do you see?
> And the Masses just suffer that Law,
> Oh dear me!
> If the rich rob the poor,
> It's quite (L) awful, I'm sure,
> But it's Ass Law as pure
> As can be …
>
> A theft by the poor is a criminal act;
> That's quite plain!
> A rich thief is only a kleptomaniac,
> Not the same.
> The poor steal in their need,
> But the rich rob for greed
> Though the Law says, 'indeed
> That's no shame!'

'UP AGAINST A STONE WALL'

This was Ernest Kavanagh's first cartoon to specifically attack William Martin Murphy, appearing on the front page of *The Irish Worker* almost a full year before the Dublin Lockout. It is a remarkably hard-hitting cartoon, depicting Larkin's Union as a stone wall closing in around a trapped Murphy, whose chariot hurtles towards an inevitable collision with the Irish Transport Workers' Union (i.e. the ITGWU, whose slogan 'An Injury to One is the Concern of All' is on display). Sitting calmly beside his bulging bags of money which have been 'plundered from the workers', Murphy whips his exhausted horses while trampling the babies and womenfolk of the workers to death. Although his features might seem calm, the clouds of dust about him indicate the frantic nature of Murphy's exit, with his sweaty and snorting horses clearly as overworked as the labourers who had fallen victim to his 'treacherous instincts'.

The cartoon accompanied a poem by an anonymous contributor, from which the following extract is taken:

> His power in finance may be prime;
> His conscience may be clogged in slime;
> He may have wealth to buy this town –
> This wall he can't be buying.
>
> So in his buggy there he sits,
> The while his yellow teeth he grits;
> He'd blow the wall up to the sky
> And with it Jimmy Larkin.
>
> For Larkin gives poor Murphy fits,
> And Bill would smash Jim into bits –
> If he could do it on the sly;
> The sweater, William Murphy.

I.T.W.U.   versus   U.W.T.I.

IRISH TRANSPORT WORKERS' UNION.   UGLY WILLIAM'S TREACHEROUS INSTINCTS.

'STEPHEN THE STUFFER OR STUFFING BY HAND'

Published in *The Irish Worker* on 9 November 1912, this cartoon attacks Stephen J. Hand, the public official in charge of maintaining and purifying the Dublin Municipal Register at the Town Clerk's Office in City Hall. Kavanagh clearly suggests that Hand, despite his enormous salary, was not doing this job properly, a view consistent with *The Irish Worker*'s line. As a former organiser for the United Irish League, the paper suspected Hand 'of acquiescence in the "stuffing" of the register with bogus voters by the registration agents of the United Irish League and of complicity in the efforts of these agents to have Labour activists disfranchised'.[10] Following the formation of the Dublin Labour Party in 1911, *The Irish Worker* was determined to maximise the chances of Labour candidates in forthcoming Municipal and Poor Law Elections. This saw the paper regularly seek to educate its readers on the practice of 'stuffing', i.e. the way in which some political party agent landlords inaccurately filled out household registration forms, 'stuffing' them with 'bogus voters'. Kavanagh's cartoon implies that Hand, along with the Lord Mayor of Dublin, Lorcan Sherlock, and the town clerk at City Hall, turned a blind eye to this illegal practice, leading to election results that were not fully reflective of public opinion.

---

10   See Peter Murray, 'Electoral Politics and the Dublin Working Class before the First World War', in *Saothar* 6 (1980), p. 12.

'ADVICE TO INTENDING APPLICANTS FOR THE SICK BENEFIT'

Published in *The Irish Worker* on 8 February 1913, this cartoon sees Kavanagh, no doubt drawing upon his own experience as a clerk in the ITGWU's National Insurance department at Liberty Hall, comically convey the cynicism traditionally associated with applications for sick benefit. Kavanagh was attempting to reveal with this cartoon how Irish workers had to lie and demean themselves in order to claim sick benefit, even when they had a valid claim. The cartoon appeared above a short advert for the ITGWU's National Insurance Approved Society, established the previous year, which insisted that all genuine sick claims would be quickly processed and looked on favourably. *The Irish Worker* called for the workers of Ireland to transfer immediately to one of the ITGWU's various insurance branches which had been set up across the country, thereby no longer having to resort to the farce of employing 'plausible lies' and 'the "cough and groan" business', depicted in Kavanagh's cartoon, if they hoped to make successful claims for sick benefit in the future.

UNTITLED ('THE DEMON OF DEATH')

Published in *The Irish Worker* on 6 September 1913, this was the first cartoon attacking William Martin Murphy during the course of the Dublin Lockout and appeared just days following the notorious 'Bloody Sunday' riot on Sackville Street. It is arguably one of Kavanagh's most powerful and memorable cartoons, depicting Murphy as a murderous vulture perched atop the entrance to his Dartry Hall home in Rathmines, south Dublin. Lying prostrate in a pool of blood outside the mansion's locked front gates is the body of a Dublin worker. The implication is clearly that Murphy had blood on his hands and was responsible for the death of several workers on Dublin's streets at the hands of the DMP. The cartoon was accompanied by a 'slightly altered' set of lines taken from Lord Byron's celebrated poem 'The Destruction of Sennacherib':

> The Demon of Death spread his wings on the blast,
> And spat on the face of the poor as he passed.[11]

During the Askwith Inquiry, set up by the British government in early October 1913 to try to secure a resolution to the Dublin Lockout, Murphy's lawyer Timothy Healy brandished the 6 September issue of *The Irish Worker* featuring Kavanagh's front-page cartoon as evidence of the persecution that his client regularly faced in Larkin's newspaper. In the same court session Murphy added his personal belief that *The Irish Worker* was an 'incitement to murder'.[12]

---

11 The correct lines in Byron's poem read 'For the Angel of Death spread his wings on the blast/And breathed in the face of the foe as he passed'.
12 See Yeates, *Lockout*, pp. 194–5.

'HIS MAJESTY IN BLUE'

Adorning the front page of *The Irish Worker* on 13 September 1913, two weeks after the 'Bloody Sunday' riot on Sackville Street, this cartoon viciously criticises the Dublin police. Sporting aggressive, imbecilic features on his ape-like face, a DMP officer – clearly drunk on both power and whiskey – triumphantly wields a bloody baton. Surrounded by bodies and broken furniture the message is clear: the Dublin police were guilty of carrying out a shameful campaign of tyranny against the working class of their city. The dust cloud behind the figure symbolises the explosive consequences of this tyranny while the way in which the word Dublin is depicted is also significant, with the broken sequence of letters implying that the chaos and disruption recently seen across the capital was due to the DMP's actions.

A short poem by 'Oscar', from which the following extract is taken, accompanied the illustration:

> His bravery is what I most admire
> To speak of which I never, never tire;
> I've seen him in a riot and, my word!
> Those rowdy people certainly were 'stirred,'
> For he can deal as well with grown-up men
> As baton ragged urchins under ten.
> His critics ask what beggar has a chance
> 'Gainst six feet of colossal ignorance?

'PITY THE POOR "BLIND" EMPLOYERS'

This cartoon was published in *The Irish Worker* on 4 October 1913, the same issue in which another Kavanagh cartoon appeared prominently on the front page, depicting William Martin Murphy directing the Dublin police to attack working-class citizens while a gallery of uncaring politicians enjoyed the spectacle. Appearing six weeks into the Dublin Lockout, it shows the Irish Transport and General Workers' Union in confident mood. A well-dressed union member, defiantly sporting his ITGWU Red Hand badge, looks on amusedly at a dishevelled and ragged Murphy, whose appeal for funds from other leading employers is clearly not having the desired response. During the Lockout the ITGWU received substantial financial funding from the British Trade Union Congress, as well as public donations from across Ireland, Britain and further afield. Approximately £150,000 was donated to the Dublin strikers' relief fund during the Lockout, a figure vastly superior to that raised by the Dublin Employers' Federation.[13] As Murphy himself admitted as early as 7 November 1913, most Dublin employers were simply 'unable to give any very large monetary assistance' to their colleague's fund due to the enormous financial strain which the Lockout was having on their businesses.[14]

---

13   O'Connor, *James Larkin*, p. 48.
14   Yeates, *Lockout*, p. 376.

'ON THE ROCKS'

Published in *The Irish Worker* on 9 November 1913, this cartoon implies that a split could emerge between Murphy and the Dublin Employers' Federation over his obsession with destroying Larkin and the ITGWU, i.e. that their relationship could be 'on the rocks'. The cartoon shows a small band of employers abandoning an enraged Murphy, leaving him stranded alone on a South Pacific island as they return to their ship without its captain. This came on the back of the largely failed attempt by the ITGWU to co-operate in sending groups of 'Dublin Kiddies' who were most affected by the Lockout to temporary British foster homes, a campaign which foundered in the face of enormous opposition from the Catholic Church and mainstream press.

Kavanagh's cartoon has two other implications: firstly, that it was Murphy rather than the children of locked-out Dublin workers who should be 'deported' from Ireland; secondly, that it was Murphy who stood in the way of any successful attempts to negotiate a fair and equitable settlement to the Lockout. Of all the items on the desolate island outcrop which are used to depict Murphy's negative legacies, the book entitled 'How to sweat employees' is perhaps most significant. The fact that it is labelled as 'Volume I' implies that it is important for the other Dublin employers to take control of the increasingly disastrous situation at this point and stage a 'mutiny', thereby putting an end to Murphy's exploitation of the city's workers which would only succeed in ruining their reputations as well as his own.

On a side-note, Ernest Kavanagh's older brother John was 'lost at sea in the North Atlantic Ocean' just six days before this cartoon was published, something which the artist was almost certainly not aware of at the time.[15] John Kavanagh, referred to as 'Jack' by his family, was thirty-six years old at the time of his death.

---

15 Cavanagh, *Soul and Clay*, p. 1.

'COMPLIMENTS OF THE SEASON'

Published in *The Irish Worker* on 3 January 1914, this cartoon sees Kavanagh depict William Martin Murphy, dressed as Santa Claus, gleefully handing out his Christmas gifts of starvation, disease and eviction to the long-suffering children of a typically crumbling Dublin slum. It appeared alongside another smaller 'E.K.' cartoon showing a similar scene of city poverty contrasted with a sketch of a self-contented Murphy enjoying his life of luxury at Dartry Hall.

'LORCAN'S WHITEWASHING'

Published on the front page of *The Irish Worker* on 10 January 1914, this cartoon attacks the Lord Mayor of Dublin for his attempts to excuse the conduct of the Dublin police. Lorcan G. Sherlock looks ludicrous dressed in his oversized robe, a sign that he did not deserve to be re-elected in the forthcoming

mayoral election, as he whitewashes a delighted DMP Constable at Glasnevin Cemetery. The latter figure's brandished baton remains ready to inflict further destruction. Two weeks later, at a 'rowdy and acrimonious city council meeting', Sherlock overcame accusations that he had 'betrayed' Dublin's workers and secured re-election.[16] On 16 February the Dublin Disturbances Commission published their report into the violence witnessed in the city, and it fully exonerated the Dublin police's conduct on 30–31 August 1913. It stated that, in extremely difficult circumstances, the DMP and Royal Irish Constabulary (RIC) had 'discharged their duties ... with conspicuous courage and patience ... zeal and determination', a declaration greeted with widespread cynicism across Ireland.[17]

---

16 Yeates, *Lockout*, pp. 526–7.
17 *Ibid.*, p. 552.

'BLUDGEONS AND BLARNEY'

This cartoon appeared in *The Irish Worker* on 30 May 1914, three weeks after Ernest Kavanagh's letter to the paper described the DMP as a criminal mob of 'murderous ruffians'.[18] It is once again fiercely critical of brutal police tactics against Dublin's poor. The cartoon shows an ape-like DMP officer enthusiastically bounding towards a group of protesting workers and their families. With his baton drawn, he urges a stiff RIC auxiliary to follow his example and commence with an indiscriminate batoning of the crowd. Kavanagh's cartoon accompanied a poem by a contributor called 'Batonio', from which the following extract is taken:

> I'm the guardian o' pace in this throublesome town,
> I'm as dhreaded as dhreaded can be;
> Whin I'm not bein' abused – well, I'm probably boozed –
> So ye'd best take example by me.
>
> I'm the terror of all the small boys that I meet,
> An' I'm most to be feared whin I laugh;
> An' betwixt porther-pulls an' the smashin' o' skulls
> I'm kept pretty busy – not half.

---

18 *The Irish Worker*, 9 May 1914. See Appendix 2 for the full text of this letter.

'Birrell's Bloody Bullies'

This cartoon was published in *The Irish Worker* on 1 August 1914, just days after the famous Howth gun-running by the Irish Volunteers had led to three civilians being shot dead by British troops in Dublin's city centre. The cartoon was dedicated to the memory of these victims – one of whom, Patrick Quinn, was an ITGWU member; another, Mary Duffy, was the wife of an ITGWU member – as well as the union members who had been killed during the opening weeks of the previous year's Dublin Lockout. The following caption accompanied the cartoon, attacking William Martin Murphy for his role in the latest tragedy:

> Lest ye forget! Murphy ordered civilian passengers out of his cars to facilitate Birrell's hired assassins and the police in their ignoble attempt to disarm Irishmen. These sweepings of Scotch slums shot down unarmed men, women and children.

The cartoon was later republished in *Cartoons. Ernest Kavanagh ('E.K.') of 'The Worker'*, minus the caption and dedication.

The Anti-Recruitment and Nationalist Cartoons

'The New Nationalism'

This cartoon was published on the front page of the August 1912 issue of *Irish Freedom*, ridiculing Irish politicians William O'Brien, John Redmond and John Dillon for learning the lyrics of patriotic British songs and turning their back on Ireland. Cathal MacDowell claimed that this 'foreshadowed the later attitude of these politicians towards Ireland and the British Empire',[1] a view shared by the *Catholic Bulletin* journal which highlighted the cartoon as a prime example of the occasionally 'prophetic' nature of Ernest Kavanagh's work.[2]

---

1   *Cartoons. Ernest Kavanagh*, p. 1.
2   *Catholic Bulletin*, December 1917, p. 780.

'THE IRISH VOLUNTEERS AND WOMEN'

Published on the front page of the *Irish Citizen* on 16 May 1914, this cartoon criticises the Irish Volunteers for the organisation's refusal to award women an equal and proper place. As suggested by its accompanying caption, the cartoon takes its inspiration from comments which had appeared in the weekly *Irish Volunteer* newspaper. The paragraph in question had been published on 21 March 1914, with the paper reporting on a recent branch meeting of the Irish Volunteers as follows:

> Mr Judge said the movement was one in which there was no room for the ladies. There was yet no need for an ambulance corps, or any other corps, but in the course of a few months there would be. Uniforms and rifles would be wanted, and these for each member would cost at least £10. There were 200,000 Volunteers in Ireland, so that would mean that they would want at least two million pounds, and the ladies could form a society, and then collect money for that, and put their hearts and souls into it (cheers).

The *Irish Citizen* reacted to those words with astonishment for the 'audacity and inconsistency' shown by M. J. Judge, a prominent Dublin nationalist and member of the Ancient Order of Hibernians, in suggesting that the Irish Volunteers did not need women, yet viewed them as crucial for the organisation's future through their collection of money.[3] The Irish Volunteer Fund had been set up on 16 December 1913 to help raise the large amount of money needed to fully equip members and satisfactorily teach them how to use arms.[4] The fact that the Irish Volunteers allowed men like Judge – who had previously earned the paper's ire by publicly suggesting that any suffragettes who harassed Prime Minister Asquith should be struck with 'slender,

---

3   *Irish Citizen*, 28 March 1914.
4   *Irish Volunteer*, 14 February 1914.

stinging, riding whips' – a prominent place on its platforms, meant the *Irish Citizen* viewed the organisation with 'considerable suspicion' and called upon it 'to recognise women's equal place in its ranks'.[5]

The gender inequality protested against by the paper is clearly evident in Kavanagh's cartoon, which depicts a smartly dressed woman holding *two* fund-raising cans towards a wealthy member of the public while a male Irish Volunteer, sporting a silly grin and twirling his moustache, stands nearby looking on.

"Mr. Judge said the movement was one in which there was no room for the ladies. . . . They would want at least two million pounds, and the ladies could form a society, and collect money for that, and put their hearts and souls into it. (Cheers)."
"Irish Volunteer."

5   *Irish Citizen*, 28 March 1914.

Untitled ('Recruiting Sergeant John Redmond')

This cartoon was published on the front page of *The Irish Worker* on 5 September 1914. It depicts John Redmond urging an Irish Volunteer to join the British war effort, thereby almost certainly ending up alongside the corpses which were already strewn across Europe's chaotic battlefields. The cartoon was accompanied by Maeve Cavanagh's poem 'England's Recruiting Jackals', which reinforced the notion that in 1914 Ireland's neighbour was a tyrannous foe to be attacked rather than a friend to be helped:

> Like a swarm of jackals hunting their prey
> The minions of England prowling go,
> The manhood and youth of Ireland to snare
> By every dastardly wile they know …
>
> Whilst the Eagle grips with the Vulture foe
> Who wrought our country's woe and decay,
> Wrest NOW from her talons your own fair land
> And grudge not Liberty's price to pay.

Recruiting Sergeant John Redmond: "The Empire (which denies you Home Rule) needs you."

'THE REDMOND – O'BRIEN PRESS GANG'

This cartoon was chosen as the front cover image of *Cartoons. Ernest Kavanagh ('E.K.') of 'The Worker'*, having initially been published on the front page of *The Irish Worker* on 26 September 1914. The cartoon shows John Redmond and William O'Brien, dressed in Napoleonic garb, dragging a clearly hesitant Irish Volunteer towards the British War Office where Lord Kitchener, Secretary of State for War, awaits to show the new recruit how to reach 'the European Shambles'. The fear on Redmond's face, that his promise to Britain regarding Irish support for the war effort will be broken unless Irish Volunteers are coerced to enlist, is clearly evident. This notion was reinforced by Maeve Cavanagh's 'The Coming of the Irish Judas and his Paymaster', which appeared beneath her brother's cartoon. This poem lambasted Redmond as a treacherous disgrace to the legacy of Wolfe Tone and Robert Emmet, insisting that the Irish Parliamentary Party leader would only ever succeed in creating an 'Irish Slaves' Brigade' made up of 'worthless curs – not men'.

'The Mansion House Recruiting Fiasco from Within'

On 25 September 1914 a high-profile recruiting meeting took place at Dublin's Mansion House with the British Prime Minister, Herbert Asquith, among the principal speakers.

At Liberty Hall the previous night a group of Irish Citizen Army men had been informed by James Larkin that, together with a section of the Irish Volunteers, they were to undertake a mission to 'take over the Mansion House and hold it so as to prevent the recruiting meeting from taking place', an announcement that 'created considerable excitement amongst those who were selected'.[6] However, the venture was called off when it emerged that the British military, anticipating such a move, had already taken the precaution of occupying the Mansion House with a large contingent of soldiers 'manned with machine guns'.[7] Yet while Larkin may not have succeeded in preventing the meeting from taking place, he was, nonetheless, in a position to have it ridiculed. He succeeded in getting Ernest Kavanagh a ticket for the event, seemingly from Thomas J. Clarke,[8] and in the 3 October issue of *The Irish Worker* 'The Mansion House Recruiting Fiasco from Within' (a cartoon subsequently described as 'dandy' by James Connolly) appeared on the front page.[9]

The cartoon features damning sketches of the main speakers and their 'protectors', the DMP and Ancient Order of Hibernians, who 'rigidly scrutinised' all those who gained admittance to the meeting. Kavanagh criticises Asquith as a liar and mocks 'Judas Empire Redmond', the 'Melancholy Humbug' John Dillon, 'the Jester' Augustine Birrell and the doddering Lord Aberdeen for the

---

6   Robbins, *Under the Starry Plough*, pp. 21–2.
7   *Ibid.*
8   Monteith, *Casement's Last Adventure*, p. 17.
9   Maeve Cavanagh MacDowell, BMH WS 258, p. 2.

The Mansion House Recruiting Fiasco from Within.

content of their speeches. The Lord Mayor of Dublin, Lorcan G. Sherlock, is depicted in the background of the Lord Aberdeen panel.

The *Catholic Bulletin* later described how the cartoon 'not only aroused the liveliest interest at the time but, in face of denials subsequently attempted, contributed to stereotype the parts played by Irish politicians in the recruitment campaign then seriously initiated'.[10] Little wonder then that 'very few recruits volunteered [to join the British army] following the meeting', which was 'somewhat of a failure'.[11] In an article that appeared alongside Kavanagh's cartoon and mocked the 'fiasco', *The Irish Worker* declared that Dublin was 'as true as ever to Ireland. The British garrison and their West British allies may say as they like, but they can go elsewhere for recruits'.[12]

---

10 *Catholic Bulletin*, December 1917, p. 781.
11 Novick, *Conceiving Revolution*, p. 193.
12 *Irish Worker*, 3 October 1914.

'JUDAS' MARCH ON WEXFORD!'

This cartoon was published on the front page of *The Irish Worker* on 10 October 1914. Drawn on the occasion of a Wexford recruitment meeting of Irish Volunteers by John Redmond the previous week, Kavanagh's cartoon offers a cruel and mocking representation of the event. Looking utterly ludicrous atop his wooden hobby-horse in a child's uniform, Redmond is cheered on by a motley crowd of supporters. These include the United Irish League leader William O'Brien, City Hall's Stephen Hand, and the Lord Mayor of Dublin Lorcan G. Sherlock. The cartoon was accompanied by a satirical poem from 'Oscar', entitled 'The Ragtime Volunteers', which completed the image of Redmond as a pathetic leader who was out of his depth and unable to persuade any Irishmen of consequence to enlist for the British army in 1914:

> They came from every public house
> Where they had been for years,
> They bid their boozing pals goodbye
> And tried to stem the tears
> That trickled down their Sunday suits
> And knocked the polish off their boots –
> The Ragtime Volunteers.

'THE ONE BRIGHT SPOT'

This cartoon appeared on the front page of *The Irish Worker* on 7 November 1914, beneath acting editor James Connolly's slogan 'We Serve Neither King Nor Kaiser'. It depicts Redmond being booted out of Ireland. Looking on unimpressed is the British Prime Minister, Herbert Asquith, who in the caption accompanying the cartoon rebukes Redmond with the words 'Like all scabs, Redmond, you are a failure from a business standpoint'. The clever title refers to the famous line by the British secretary of state for foreign affairs, upon Britain's entry into the First World War on 3 August 1914, that Ireland was 'the one bright spot on the horizon'. This statement was warmly endorsed by Redmond, who promised that Ireland would show herself worthy of such praise and support Britain, rather than seeking to take advantage of her difficulty as on former occasions.[13] Three months later, with the enlistment figures of Irish soldiers far below what both Redmond and Asquith had hoped, Kavanagh's cartoon jeers the Irish Parliamentary Party leader for his failure to back up these words and deliver on his promise.

13   See A. C. Hepburn (ed.), *Ireland 1905–1925. Volume 2: Documents and Analysis* (Newtownards 1998), p. 139.

'THE COMING OF THE HUN'

Kavanagh's last cartoon to be published in *The Irish Worker* before its suppression, this appeared on the front page on 21 November 1914. It offers an indirect indictment of Ireland's involvement in the First World War, depicting 'John Bull' refusing General Kitchener's call for him to become one of the further million 'mugs wanted to stop German bullets', even when the threat of 'The Hun' was on his very own doorstep. Kavanagh makes clear *The Irish Worker*'s view that wealthy Englishmen had no interest in joining the 'gallant troops' getting chased across Europe by the 'cowardly' enemy, instead choosing to simply ignore the war and carry on with their business affairs as normal.

'PARTITION'

This cartoon was published posthumously in the December 1917 issue of the *Catholic Bulletin*, the journal praising the cartoon for showing 'a far-seeing appreciation of the Partition proposals'.[14] It also subsequently re-appeared in *Cartoons. Ernest Kavanagh ('E.K.') of 'The Worker'* under the caption 'The Nation Mutilators'. In the cartoon John Redmond and Edward Carson are depicted as joining forces to ignore the pleas of Ireland by cutting part of Ulster off from the rest of the country. By opposing Ireland's partition Kavanagh was taking the official ITGWU line. When Redmond reluctantly agreed to the British government's plans to temporarily exclude part of the province of Ulster in an amended Home Rule Bill in 1914, *The Irish Worker* lambasted the Irish Parliamentary Party leader and the other 'pygmy statesmen' who were seen to be betraying Ireland.[15]

---

14 *Catholic Bulletin*, December 1917, p. 780.
15 *Irish Worker*, 21 March 1914.

'A LONG, LONG WAY TO BERLIN'

Two weeks after the suppression of *The Irish Worker* James Connolly published the first and only issue of *Irish Work*, which appeared with the tagline 'Published When the Censor Wasn't Looking'. This provocative cartoon appeared on its front page, the only instance of one of Kavanagh's cartoons appearing without a signature. Connolly made this decision for Kavanagh's protection, but the artist was said to be 'anything but grateful'.[16] In the cartoon Germany is depicted as humiliating Britain on the battlefields of Flanders as 1914 draws to a close. With his rifle by his side as he smokes a cigarette, an Irish Volunteer enjoys the spectacle and rather than intervening wants to add to 'John Bull's woes. The title of the cartoon, later revealed in *Cartoons. Ernest Kavanagh ('E.K.') of 'The Worker'*, was a reference to the famous Allied marching song 'A Long Way to Tipperary'. It suggests that Britain faced an enormous task in forcing the German army back to Berlin and winning the war, with Ireland clearly not willing to offer any assistance.

JOHN BULL—" Help! my brave Hirish."
IRISH VOLUNTEER—" After you with the ' Cat,' Fritz."

---

16 *Cartoons. Ernest Kavanagh*, p. 2; Maeve Cavanagh MacDowell, BMH WS 258, p. 2.

'The Shade of Wolfe Tone'

This illustration appeared in *Cartoons. Ernest Kavanagh ('E.K.') of 'The Worker'*, having earlier been published as a postcard in 1915. It shows the ghost of Wolfe Tone pointing an accusing finger at John Redmond and John Dillon, two salaried Irish MPs who are depicted as cowardly traitors. Like the rest of his family, Ernest Kavanagh was a great admirer of Wolfe Tone. In 1913 he drew a portrait of the United Irishmen's founder, presenting it to the Wolfe Tone Memorial Committee 'for the purpose of raising funds'.[17]

---

17   *Cartoons. Ernest Kavanagh*, p. 2. The president of the Wolfe Tone Memorial Committee was Thomas J. Clarke, a friend of Ernest Kavanagh's.

'BULMER HOBSON, AN IRISH VOLUNTEER, AND JOHN BULL'

Unpublished in Kavanagh's lifetime, this illustration subsequently appeared in *Cartoons. Ernest Kavanagh ('E.K.') of 'The Worker'*. In the introduction Cathal MacDowell noted that Kavanagh looked upon Bulmer Hobson and Eoin MacNeill as 'bluffers' rather than men who had the courage to fight for Irish independence.[18] In relation to Hobson, such a view is made clear by this cartoon. He is dismissed as 'Babbler Codsome' – a man who was all talk and no action – and depicted as desperate for the Irish Volunteers not to take advantage of England's difficulty in the First World War by launching a rebellion against their foe. Although Hobson might gripe about the 'Foul Saxon' in *Irish Freedom*, the weekly nationalist newspaper he edited which was 'the unacknowledged organ of the IRB', Kavanagh wanted to expose him in this cartoon as nothing more than a 'tin' revolutionary, a man who would never have the courage to 'consummate the great task' and actually lead a rebellion against British rule.[19]

---

18   *Cartoons. Ernest Kavanagh*, p. 1.
19   Bulmer Hobson, *Ireland Yesterday and Tomorrow* (Anvil Books Limited 1968), p. 42.

99

'BULMER HOBSON AND THE PEELER'

This is another unpublished cartoon attacking Hobson which posthumously appeared in *Cartoons. Ernest Kavanagh ('E.K.') of 'The Worker'*. With his silly grin, grotesque nose and dwarfish physique, Hobson cuts a small and pathetic figure as he politely asks an amused DMP constable for permission to stage a revolution. The cartoon clearly emphasises the view that Hobson was a timid disgrace to the legacy of Wolfe Tone. Maeve Cavanagh shared her brother's disdain for Hobson, convinced that he 'would never do anything decisive' despite his regular attacks in print against the British.[20]

A defiant Hobson later insisted that it was only 'a decisive defeat' which he was opposed to. He was convinced that Irish nationalists should seek to 'paralyse the administration with passive resistance' rather than following James Connolly and Patrick Pearse's foolish plan of locking 'bodies of men up in a number of buildings to stay there until they were shot or burned out'.[21]

The cartoon is undated but was most likely drawn at some stage during the opening months of 1916.

---

20 Maeve Cavanagh MacDowell, BMH WS 258, p. 5.
21 Hobson, *Ireland Yesterday and Tomorrow*, pp. 73, 75.

'THE HOMEWARD TRAIL'

Although only a 'rough sketch and not intended for publication', this illustration was later included in *Cartoons. Ernest Kavanagh ('E.K.') of 'The Worker'*, with Cathal MacDowell feeling that it was 'one of the most telling' cartoons that his brother-in-law had ever produced. Drawn shortly before Kavanagh's death, the cartoon shows a German officer taunting England for her failure to successfully 'protect' Belgium, Serbia and Montenegro in the opening two years of the First World War. An Irish Volunteer looks on as a wounded and battered 'John Bull', whose 'figure and expression' earned praise from MacDowell, limps home in disgrace.[22] The cartoon's caption reinforces the message that if the Irish Volunteers now showed courage and took advantage of England's current difficulty, then Ireland's foe would soon be 'finished'.

---

22   *Cartoons. Ernest Kavanagh*, p. 2.

THE SUFFRAGE CARTOONS

'THE ANGEL OF FREEDOM'

This cartoon was published on the front page of the *Irish Citizen* newspaper on 15 March 1913. It is one of Kavanagh's most famous illustrations, depicting John Redmond as a hypocrite who campaigned for national emancipation while simultaneously opposing the right of Irishwomen to have the vote. The paper was extremely proud of the cartoon and urged its readers 'to let the official Nationalist politicians see copies of it' during that week's St Patrick's Day celebrations.[1] It was also later issued in postcard form.[2] When the House of Commons met on 6 May 1913 to discuss a Women's Suffrage Bill, the London correspondent of the *Freeman's Journal* and *Evening Telegraph* reported the following day on how:

> By yesterday's post leading Irishmen of different parties received from Dublin copies of a most offensive suffragist cartoon, in which Mr John Redmond, caricatured as 'An Angel of Freedom', is depicted trampling on a bound and prostrate female, and bearing in his right hand a paper inscribed 'Hurro for Liberty'.[3]

The *Irish Citizen* ridiculed this report and claimed that the only thing 'offensive' about the cartoon had been its exposure of 'one of the most glaring political offenses of all time'.[4] Although the paper reported that the publicity they were given by the mainstream press led to an increase in their sales, this was a minor victory. The Dickenson's Women's Suffrage Bill was defeated in the House of

---

1   *Irish Citizen*, 15 March 1913.
2   NLI, Sheehy-Skeffington papers, Ms 41,201/10.
3   *Freeman's Journal*, 7 May 1913; *Evening Telegraph*, 7 May 1913.
4   *Irish Citizen*, 24 May 1913.

Commons by 266 to 219 votes, with only a fraction of the Irish MPs who were in attendance during the debate voting in favour of the bill.

'THE SUFFRAGETTE SCARE IN DUBLIN'

Wonderfully capturing the hysteria still gripping the Irish authorities following bomb-scares in Dublin some weeks earlier, this cartoon appeared on the front page of the *Irish Citizen* on 31 May 1913. The paper believed that the most serious of these scares had been 'deliberately planned with a view to discrediting the Suffragist Movement in Dublin', and was aghast at how irresponsible it believed the mainstream press was in reporting on both this and countless bomb hoaxes carried out across Dublin by 'schoolboys and other persons with a turn for primitive humour'.[5] Kavanagh depicts a foolish member of the DMP's 'Intilligence Department' instructing a young police officer, who is positively shaking with fear, to arrest what he believes to be a 'Disguised Militant Selling Bombs'. In reality, it is clear that this so-called terrorist is simply a poor, working-class woman selling Spanish onions at a Dublin street corner.

Discovery by the Intilligince Department of a Disguised Militant Selling Bombs

5   *Irish Citizen*, 24 May 1913.

'HER MASTER'S VOICE'

Published on the front page of the *Irish Citizen* on 6 September 1913, this cartoon requires very little comment. It clearly seeks to demonstrate the injustice of allowing men to continue to prevent women from having the right to vote on the foolish assumption that they were 'physically and mentally' inferior beings. The cartoon was published on the same day that Kavanagh's famous depiction of William Martin Murphy as a vulture outside his Dartry Hall mansion appeared on the front page of *The Irish Worker*.

" Ma dear fella, we caun't give Votes to Women.   They are physically and mentally our inferiors."

Appendix 1

Cartoons by other Artists

In order to provide a visual comparison and contrast to Ernest Kavanagh's work, the following short selection of cartoons by contemporary artists has been included.

'To Him that Hath Shall be Given'

This cartoon appeared on the front page of *The Irish Worker* on 23 December 1911. It is arguably one of 'C.B.'s most powerful cartoons to have been published in the paper, presenting a scene in which a pair of bare-footed and ragged 'slum children' plead in vain for Christmas presents from Santa Claus as they wander snow-covered streets. Child-related propaganda was a regular feature of *The Irish Worker*'s pages.

Slum Children—Have you Nothing at all for us?
Santa Claus—Sorry, dears, but your names are not on my list. You have been forgotten again.

'Our Overworked Police – A Snap-Shot'

Published in *The Irish Worker* on 30 December 1911, this cartoon sees 'C.B.' poke fun at three lazy and overweight DMP officers who are smoking tobacco and drinking alcohol while on duty. This was typical of the regular jabs taken against the DMP which appeared in the paper at the time. Ernest Kavanagh later produced cartoons of increased venom about the city's police during the Dublin Lockout, depicting them as corrupt, drunken, murderous bullies who abused their power and were wildly out of control. This escalating hostility reflected the overall attitude of *The Irish Worker* towards the Dublin police, especially following the 'Bloody Sunday' riot and other examples of police violence witnessed in late August 1913.

'THE REAL STRIKERS'

This cartoon by 'Spex' (John Fergus O'Hea) appeared in the October 1913 issue of the Dublin-based *Lepracaun* journal. Bearing a striking resemblance to Ernest Kavanagh's 'His Majesty in Blue', which had been published in *The Irish Worker* the previous month, it is an incredibly powerful and disturbing cartoon. O'Hea severely reproaches the Dublin police for the brutal and seemingly indiscriminate baton attacks carried out across the city during the opening days of the Lockout. The cartoon was accompanied by the following caption:

> On August 30 and 31 the Dublin Metropolitan Police and the R. I. Constabulary ran 'amok' in the City of Dublin. Result: Two men batoned to death and several hundred men, women and children badly beaten, whose ages range from one week to ninety years.

The two fatalities referred to were Dublin labourers James Nolan and John Byrne, who died as a result of horrific head injuries suffered during riots in the early days of the Lockout. The one-week-old victim was accidentally given a black eye during a police ransacking of her widowed mother's tenement home.[6]

---

6   Greaves, *Irish Transport and General Workers' Union*, p. 99.

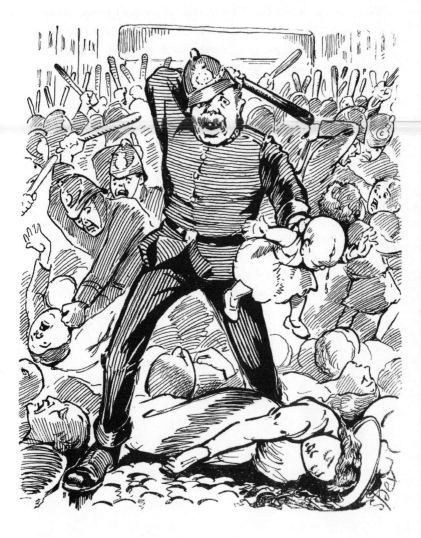

'DUBLIN, OCTOBER, 1913'

This cartoon by 'Spex' (John Fergus O'Hea) appeared in the October issue of the *Lepracaun*, offering a neutral perspective of the Dublin Lockout. The cartoon depicts a corpulent employer and muscular worker, both of whom have their shirts rolled up and are clearly spoiling for a fight, stubbornly threatening each other with their respective weapons of the lockout and strike. As can be seen in the background, the result is an inevitable closure of factories across Dublin and an overflowing of the city's workhouses. A brief caption beneath the cartoon lamented how there was 'at present an army of over 20,000 unemployed in the City of Dublin', a clear warning as to how dangerous it would be if the great industrial deadlock was allowed to continue any longer in its current form. The following month O'Hea produced another similar cartoon, 'Flattening Him Out', which implied even more forcefully that it was the general public who were 'getting the worst of it' and suffering far more than either the employers or locked-out trade unionists in 1913.

DUBLIN, OCTOBER, 1913.

'THE AUNT SALLY'

Published in the *Lepracaun*'s August 1913 issue, this cartoon sees 'S.H.Y.' depict James Larkin as a figure who didn't 'care tuppence' about the ordinary people of Dublin and deserved to be treated with 'stern measures'. The ITGWU general secretary is portrayed as a self-serving 'strike monger', somebody who was just as harmful for the welfare of Dublin's citizens as the high-rent charging landlords, expensive food merchants and unaccountable rate comptrollers whom he was fond of attacking on their behalf. 'Aunt Sally' was a traditional fairground throwing game at the time, and is a metaphorical term commonly used to mean someone or something that is a target for criticism.

THE AUNT SALLY.

(1)—AS IT IS.

(2)—AS IT OUGHT TO BE.

'IN THE IRISH ZOO'

Published in the 1913 Christmas Number issue of the *Lepracaun*, this cartoon compilation sees 'S.H.Y.' provide a selection of animal-inspired cartoon representations of some of Ireland's most recognisable public figures from the time. Each cartoon was accompanied by a rhyming couplet, with the entire collection introduced as follows:

> Kind friends, if you're not very busy today,
> A trip to the Zoo come with me and pay;
> Come with me and see each in his own cage,
> The wonderful beasts of this wonderful age.

Several of the figures featured also appeared in many of Ernest Kavanagh's cartoons, including Lorcan Sherlock, William O'Brien, John Redmond, William Martin Murphy and James Larkin. The latter two representations are included here. The first sees 'S.H.Y.' portray Murphy as a proud, ferocious and hungry lion. The bone clutched in his paws refers to Murphy's staunch opposition earlier that year to the projected building of an art gallery beside the River Liffey, which was to house a large donation of valuable French paintings from Sir Hugh Lane. Murphy led the public opposition of Dublin's elite, arguing that the gallery would only prove to be a tremendous waste of taxpayer's money and provide the city with a facility that would not 'be of the smallest use to the common people'.[7] Larkin and *The Irish Worker* opposed this stance, believing that an art gallery would help to give the Dublin's beleaguered working-class population an appreciation of culture. This argument is not referenced in 'S.H.Y.'s representation of Larkin as a ruinous white elephant, eager to promote the breaking of all business contracts. This latter point is a clear reference to Larkin's famous declaration that contracts, in situations where the employers were clearly in the

---

7   Morrissey, *William Martin Murphy*, p. 39.

wrong, were not 'sacred' and could thus be justifiably broken by the workers.

'TIME TO DO THIS'

On 6 September 1913, the same day that Ernest Kavanagh's depiction of William Martin Murphy as a murderous vulture outside Dartry Hall appeared on the front page of *The Irish Worker*, the *Evening Herald* published this cartoon by Gordon Brewster. It shows the sturdy boot of Dublin's employers kicking James Larkin out of their city, thereby valiantly ridding it of the scourge of 'Larkinism' and the 'vicious strikes' associated with the movement. The message of the cartoon is clear: The Dublin Employers' Federation remained unrepentant in the wake of the carnage witnessed on Dublin's streets the previous weekend, with the finger of blame for the violent clashes firmly placed at Larkin's door.

'STRIKE AT THE HAUL'

'Strike at the Haul' by W. J. Miller appeared in the 6 September 1913 issue of the *Liberator and Irish Trade Unionist*, 'a scurrilous anti-Larkin paper' which appeared on the eve of the Dublin Lockout and was most likely subsidised by the Dublin Employers' Federation.[8] The cartoon is indicative of the sustained attempt by the paper to attack the honesty of '£arkin' (as he was constantly called) and accuse him of growing rich while his exploited and duped followers starved to death. It accuses the ITGWU general secretary of only looking out for himself and secretly embezzling over £2,000 from sales of *The Irish Worker*, depicted here as a vile paper filled with 'mud, abuse, blackmail, filth' that was only fit to be sold on Dublin's streets by grotesque-looking newsboys. The woman standing outside Liberty Hall with starving children, watching helplessly as Larkin strides happily away, is included to mock the struggling Irish Women Workers' Union. This organisation operated out of Liberty Hall alongside the ITGWU and had been set up in September 1911, with Larkin's sister Delia serving as its inaugural general secretary during the IWWU's first four years of existence. In fact, the woman may actually be a representation of Delia Larkin herself, who was 'the public face of Liberty Hall' at the time, following her brother's temporary departure to England.[9] During the Dublin Lockout Delia played a key role organising the distribution of food and clothes to thousands of children affected by the dispute.

---

8   O'Connor, *James Larkin*, p. 44. See also John Newsinger, "'The Devil It Was Who Sent Larkin To Ireland": The *Liberator*, Larkinism and The Dublin Lockout of 1913', in *Saothar* 18 (1993).
9   Moriarty, 'Delia Larkin', p. 433.

APPENDIX 2

LETTER BY ERNEST KAVANAGH PUBLISHED IN
THE IRISH WORKER (9 MAY 1914)

A letter appeared in the 'Irish Times' of the 1st inst., from a Colonel Moore, purporting to explain the objects of the Irish Volunteers. One portion of his letter is a real gem – viz., 'In the event of local disturbances the Irish Volunteers are expected to assist the police in maintaining peace'. This paragraph will appeal, particularly to the Irish working class, when we remember the murderous ruffians who, during the recent labour dispute in Dublin, butchered two of our fellow citizens and maimed hundreds of others, and spared neither woman [*sic*] or children. And the Irish Volunteers are 'to assist the police in maintaining peace'. The gallant colonel does not state if the Irish Volunteers are 'to assist the police' when these bloated bullies break into workingmen's homes and smash their little household effects. Neither does the Colonel mention if the Irish Volunteers will be expected to scab in the event of another lock-out. But if the gallant colonel hopes to make Irish Volunteers act as auxiliary 'polismin' it would not astonish me if he also required them to scab, for the man who would 'assist the police' in Ireland would be capable of any crime in the calendar. Now, as I believe there are a large number of workingmen in the Irish Volunteers, I respectfully suggest to them that they instantly repudiate Moore's statement in no uncertain way, otherwise the Irish Volunteers will be justly regarded with grave suspicion by all honest Nationalist workers. – Yours, &c

'E.K.'

APPENDIX 3

TRIBUTE POEMS TO HER BROTHER BY
MAEVE CAVANAGH

To 'E.K.'

When first they told me you were dead,
I scarcely felt Grief's pain,
Straight in the face I looked black dread,
And barred it from my brain.

I shed no tears, I turned to hear
Your step at every sound,
So strong your presence seemed and near
That Wonder sorrow drowned.

How strange it seemed, I saw a draft,
Your hands had just left there,
And all the small things of your craft
Beside your empty chair.

Brother and sister were we two
Comrades, soul-friends beside,
And yet how dear I hardly knew
Till now when you have died.

Death came to you in tragic guise,
Lone as your life had been;
No law your murder justifies,
Save England's laws unclean.

I think not on it lest I curse
The hand the bullet sped:
But one word 'Murdered' clear and terse
I wrote above my dead.

To every noble cause your heart
Went forth unerring, true,
Maybe you played a greater part,
And braver than you knew.

Many a hope and dream we shared,
As we worked side by side;
Brother when Death his secret bared
Was life's pain justified?

I would not dare your sleep to break
With futile praise or blame –
But this – that for your lost life's sake,
Mine ne'er shall be the same.

Published in *A Voice of Insurgency* (Dublin 1916)

***

ERNEST CAVANAGH. EASTER TUESDAY, 1916

In wood and field, spring's golden flowers are gleaming,
From their white dreams, the Easter Lilies rise,
Blackbird and thrush, unawed by your long dreaming,
Over your grave, shrill their loud melodies.

Few speak your name – save those your death left lonely;
As you would wish, who knew the worth of fame;
They keep the mind of your dread passing only,
They who knew best, your meed of praise or blame.

Each cause you served, to victory surges onward,
What if their annals keep no niche for you,
Will e'er your soul, from its great quest look backward,
Wistful, that men, withheld your little due?

Nay, you would smile your quiet smile, as ever,
Thinking of names the world remembered not;

They who had borne the torch, where light was never –
With those, 'twere more than fame to be forgot.

Published in the *Irish Opinion: Voice of Labour* newspaper
(19 April 1919)

BIBLIOGRAPHY

PRIMARY SOURCES

Newspapers/Periodicals

The Catholic Bulletin
The Evening Herald
Fianna
The Freeman's Journal
Gaelic American
Irish Citizen
Irish Freedom
Irish Opinion: Voice of Labour
Irish Press
The Irish Times
Irish Volunteer
The Irish Worker
Irish Workers' Voice
The Lepracaun
The (London) Times
The Workers' Republic

Personal Papers

William O'Brien Papers (NLI)
Maeve Cavanagh MacDowell Papers (NLI)
Sheehy-Skeffington Papers (NLI)

Bureau of Military History Witness Statements

Maeve Cavanagh MacDowell WS 258
Frank Robbins WS 585

SECONDARY SOURCES

Bew, John, *John Redmond* (Dundalk 1996)
Bracken, Pauline, *Light of Other Days. A Dublin Childhood* (Cork 1992)
Burch, Steven Dedalus, *Andrew P. Wilson and the Early Irish and Scottish National Theatres 1911–1950* (New York 2009)

Cavanagh, Maeve, *A Voice of Insurgency* (Dublin 1916)
—— *Soul & Clay* (Dublin 1917)
—— *Passion Flowers* (Dublin 1918)
Curry, James, 'Delia Larkin: More harm to the Big Fellow than any of the employers?' in *Saothar* 36 (2011), pp. 19–25
Curtis, L. Perry, *Apes and Angels: The Irishman in Victorian caricature* (revised edition, Washington & London 1997)
Devine, Francis, *Organising History: A Centenary of SIPTU, 1909–2009* (Dublin 2009)
Douglas, Roy, Harte, Liam & O'Hara, Jim, *Drawing Conclusions: A Cartoon History of Anglo-Irish Relations 1798–1998* (Belfast 1998)
Dublin Labour History Workshop, *Larkin in Perspective: from communism to evolutionary socialism* (Dublin 1983)
Fox, R. M., *Rebel Irishwomen* (Dublin 1967)
—— *Jim Larkin: the Rise of the Underman* (London 1957)
Glandon, Virginia E., *Arthur Griffith and the Advanced-Nationalist Press in Ireland, 1900–1922* (New York 1985)
Greaves, C. Desmond, *The Irish Transport and General Workers' Union: the formative years 1909–1923* (Dublin 1982)
Hansard Parliamentary Debates. Fifth Series
Hepburn, A. C. (ed.), *Ireland 1905–1925. Volume 2: Documents and Analysis* (Newtownards 1998)
Hobson, Bulmer, *Ireland Yesterday and Tomorrow* (Anvil Books Limited 1968)
Keogh, Dermot, 'William Martin Murphy and the 1913 Dublin Lockout' in *Saothar* 4 (1970)
Larkin, Emmet, *James Larkin, Irish labour leader, 1876–1947* (London 1965)
Larkin, Felix M., *Terror and Discord. The Shemus cartoons in the Freeman's Journal, 1920–1924* (Dublin 2009)
Lowery, Robert, 'Sean O'Casey and *The Irish Worker* (with an index, 1911–14)', in Lowery, Robert (ed.), *O'Casey Annual* 3 (London 1984)
Mac Giolla Choille, Breandán, *Intelligence Notes 1913–16* (Dublin 1966)
Monteith, Robert, *Casement's Last Adventure* (Chicago 1932)
Morrissey, Thomas, *William Martin Murphy* (Dundalk 1997)
Murray, Peter, 'Electoral Politics and the Dublin Working Class before the First World War', in *Saothar* 6 (1980)
Nevin, Donal (ed.), *James Larkin: lion of the fold* (Dublin 1998)
—— *Writings of James Connolly. Collected Works* (Dublin 2011)

Newsinger, John, "'The Devil It Was Who Sent Larkin To Ireland": The *Liberator*, Larkinism and The Dublin Lockout of 1913', in *Saothar* 18 (1993)

Novick, Ben, *Conceiving Revolution. Irish Nationalist Propaganda during the First World War* (Dublin 2001)

O'Casey, Sean, *Autobiographies I* (London 1963)

—— *The Story of the Irish Citizen Army* (Journeyman Press Edition 1980)

O'Connor, Emmet, *James Larkin* (Cork 2002)

Plunkett, James, *Strumpet City* (London 1969)

Robbins, Frank, *Under the Starry Plough. Recollections of the Irish Citizen Army* (Dublin 1977)

Ryan, Louise, 'The *Irish Citizen*, 1912–1920', *Saothar* 17 (1992)

Ryan, W. P., *The Irish labour movement from the 'twenties to our own day* (Dublin 1919)

Van Voris, Jacqueline, *Constance de Markievicz: in the cause of Ireland* (Amherst 1967)

Wright, Arnold, *Disturbed Dublin: the story of the great strike of 1913-14: with a description of the industries of the Irish capital* (London 1914)

Yeates, Pádraig, *Lockout: Dublin 1913* (Dublin 2000)

INDEX